W9-ABN-304

What About Religion?

An Exploratory View

Wanda Cawein

**Midnight Oil
Publishing Co.**
Eugene, Oregon
1992

For my children and yours.

Library of Congress Catalog Card Number 92-60737
ISBN 0-9633488-1-7

Book Printing:
Vesta Publishing Services
P.O. Box 5474
Eugene, Oregon 97405

Illustrations by Wanda Cawein and Diantha Morris
Book cover design by Dan Gilmore
Text editing and input by Phil Hennin

To order copies of this book:
Midnight Oil Publishing Co.
1544 Orchard Street
Eugene, Oregon 97403

Contents

Introduction

When a soft-spoken, orange-clad, shaven-headed Buddhist monk approaches you at the airport, asking for a donation; when a family of white-turbaned Sikhs pedal past you on the bike path, when *The New York Times* carries a picture of a scantily-clad Jain ascetic meditating on his bed of nails; you may experience a fleeting curiosity about these strangers. Children almost always do. Answering their questions can be difficult, not because the information isn't available; it just isn't part of what we've assimilated in our growing-up years.

Religion is an integral part of the human experience. Therefore, knowledge of religion should be included in every person's education. It isn't. As parent, teacher and guide of children for many years, I have seen that this is so. Children taught in church and temple schools usually learn about their particular church or temple only. Most of the children in public schools today have very little background in any knowledge of religion. It is difficult for parents to answer questions about world religions because they have been raised in the same kind of vacuum.

I think that young people have the right to know how and why people worship. I think they want to know, and that the knowledge will equip them better for life on an increasingly crowded and diversely populated planet.

What About Religion? doesn't pretend to be a complete encyclopaedia of religion. No one would read such a volume. What it does is to briefly review the history of worship, the rise of the priesthood, and the rebellions against corrupt priests that led to the formation of the world's most popular faiths. It isn't complete, nor does it try to be. What it does is to try to evoke some interest by discussion of some unusual and esoteric practices. It has been my experience that everyone appreciates the exotic and the bizarre.

What About Religion? is an attempt to reduce prejudice and intolerance through knowledge and understanding.

In the Beginning

What is Religion?

Although we can only guess at our beginnings, some experts say that man has existed on Earth for over 350,000 years. In spite of the fact that written proof only goes back about 5000 years when writing began, we can assume from pictures, carvings and other artifacts that man has been practicing some form of religion during most of his existence. The word, "religion," comes from the Latin word, "religio." It means "having reverence and respect for one or many gods or spirits, even though we cannot see them."

1

A person who is religious believes that a supernatural world exists and has something to do with the way our universe operates.

Every religion has at least one of the following involved in its practise: rituals to perform, rules to obey, leaders to follow, tales to narrate, formulas to recite, objects to manipulate, holy days to keep, places to frequent or avoid, natural phenomena by which to predict the future, and literature to learn from and think about. To be religious means to relate to what is sacred or holy to you in one or more of these ways.

Anthropologists, those social scientists who study the ways that groups of people behave, say that religions came to be because sharing common beliefs and practises brought ancient people closer together as they struggled to understand their experiences and learn about their origins. Celebrating mutual ceremonies made them feel more secure in a world that was full of danger and without scientific explanations. Religion gave their lives more meaning and direction.

Prehistoric Man

Imagine a time long ago, when the Earth was a huge wilderness, covered with forests and jungles, without cities, roads or cultivated fields. Roaming this wilderness were animals that were very different from those of today's world, such as wild horses and dogs, bison and shaggy mammoth elephants. The men of this Paleolithic

(Old Stone) Age of 50,000 to 150,000 years ago were probably shorter than we are and different-looking also. From the skeletons found in 1857 in the Neanderthal Valley of the Rhine River in Germany, we know that Neanderthal man had a sloping forehead, a prominent, sharply ridged brow, and huge thigh bones. Later excavations by archeologists in Java, China and Africa have produced other Neanderthal skeletons.

Excavations in Europe later produced evidence of a different prehistoric man called Cro-Magnon after the cave in France where the skeletons were found. These skeletons, which were about 30,000 years old, were of a taller people with firm chins, high foreheads and very

Neanderthal Man, as he may have looked.

prominent cheekbones. They more closely resembled modern man.

Although prehistoric man did not have a written language, he left numerous clues about his existence in the form of utensils, carved idols and reliefs, rock paintings and drawings, as well as remains of temples, altars and graves. These artifacts tell us that early man was able to reason with his brain and to create with his hands. In fact, in some cases his cave paintings were so well done that some people refused to believe that prehistoric man could have done them.

One example of this skepticism occurred in the 1870s in Spain, when Don Marcelino de Santuola, an aristocratic gentleman whose hobby was geology, discovered some extraordinarily beautiful cave paintings at Altamira. There was a whole extensive ceiling of wild horses, charging bison and boars, painted in shades of red, brown and black so skillfully that scientists of the time refused to believe that prehistoric man could have done them 50,000 years previously. These doubters were not unusual, since many of their contemporaries preferred believing that man had only been created and put on Earth in 4004 B.C. They accused Don Marcelino of being a fake, and of having had the paintings done by a French painter who had been visiting him. They realized and admitted their error only many years later, after the Don had died a very bitter and unhappy man.

Like the Altamira paintings, other prehistoric drawings and carvings of bone, ivory and stone usually depicted animals. This was probably because Stone Age man was a hunter who depended on animals for food and clothing, and so they were an essential part of his everyday life. They were also one of the natural phenomena that man did not yet control and so, like the rain, sun, thunder and lightning, man began to religiously imbue animals with spirits that he respected and asked for help in times of need. At that time it was believed that creating images enabled a man to have some control over the soul of whatever was represented, so animals were often depicted. Sometimes they were painted to be pregnant so there would be more plentiful herds for hunting. As recently as 1940, paintings of bison, cattle and mammoths were discovered by children playing in the caves of Lascaux in southern France. Carbon dating has proven these paintings to be about 15,000 years old.

The Carbon-14 method of dating artifacts is reliable up to works of 50,000 years ago and is most effective with samples of wood or charcoal. The method employs Carbon-14, a radioactive element that is absorbed by all living things at a steady rate while they live. When they die, the intake of Carbon-14 stops and what is accumulated begins to break down. Because we know the breakdown rate (called half-life) of elements, we can measure the amount of Carbon-14 in organic substances and tell when an organism died.

Cave paintings and drawings of the Mesolithic (Middle Stone) Age, 15,000 to 5,000 years ago, reveal that domestication of animals by man began at that time.

It is probable that the dog was one of the first animals to be controlled by man, followed by the horse, the ox, sheep, goat and pig. It is believed that the wolf, ancestor of the dog, used to hang around the camps of hunters to feed on the discarded remains of hunted animals. Although large, strong wolves were chased away, the smaller ones were encouraged to stay, to scavenge, and to act as watchdogs who would set up a howl when dangerous strangers or other animals approached the camp. Sometimes they were used to chase down and exhaust herds of animals like deer for the kill.

Man and his domesticated wolf/dog learned to appreciate and revere the power of fire during the Stone Age. Evidence indicates that the dead were often buried near the hearth, perhaps for comfort. However, because fire could scorch and cause pain as well, man considered it the dwelling place of a powerful god. With respect, he worshipped this natural phenomenon.

Along with fire, each power of nature in a complex world became associated with its own god. These gods together ruled over man and the Earth. They were thought to take the form of animals sometimes and visit Earth; this belief evolved into the worship of animals. These animal gods were often worshipped communally as settlements developed, and were thought to be responsible for whole groups of people. Among the animals later worshipped by the ancient Egyptians were the cat, the ibis bird and the crocodile. Egyptians also revered a bull of a particular color that to them represented their Nile River, the main source of their water. The special Bull Apis, chosen one at a time, was treated as royalty, waited on by priests, kept in a luxurious stable, and mourned by all the people of the kingdom when he died, after which a successor Bull Apis would be chosen.

Natural Phenomena

In the Neolithic (New Stone) Age of 5,000 to 10,000 years ago, archeological digs reveal that man began to settle down and raise crops. Like the hunters before him, the early farmer living in a small tribal society led a difficult life that was heavily dependent on natural phenomena. Along with the spirits of animals, he came to revere the spirits of plants, the sun, and the rain that he needed for raising his food. Because so much of the influence came from the sky, he began to look upward to the heavens as the home of gods. The causes of thunder and lightning, earthquakes, tornadoes, eclipses and floods were incomprehensible to him, and so he was kept in awe and fear of the spirits that he believed controlled these happenings.

To give an example, one group of ancient people came out of Asia and settled in what is now known as Egypt along the 3000-mile Nile River. The Nile would flood the land every spring, leaving behind fertile soil when it receded; this was one natural phenomenon that the Egyptians considered a sacred mystery. They believed that their world was a long flat oval divided by the Nile and surrounded by mountains, around which flowed the Heavenly River. In this river, the Sun God sailed daily in his Heavenly Boat until sunset, when he would be hidden by the mountains during the hours of darkness. Because the Nile had six great cataracts that prevented early Egyptians from exploring the headwaters, they believed the river flowed to them through a cleft in the mountains from a sacred cavern, home of the spirit of the river.

To stay on the right side of such powerful spirits and gods, man began to build altars on which to make sacrifices to them. These offerings were given to thank the gods for prosperous times, to ask their help in times of trouble, and to appease them when they were thought to be angry. Sacrifices took the form of food, animals, and sometimes human lives. Since people knew that blood was essential to life, they would sometimes shed this blood of animals or humans in order to be making the ultimate sacrifice.

As ancient man observed the natural phenomena of the heavens, the stars, the planets and other moving heavenly bodies, he interpreted their movements as spiritual signs by which he could predict the future. The Persians of Asia Minor and the Chaldeans of Babylonia used the heavenly movements both to make predictions and to reveal to them events of great importance. It is believed to have been Chaldeans who were the three Magi or Wise Men who traveled to Bethlehem to see the newborn Jesus Christ, the birth of whom they claimed to have read in the stars. The moon (meaning "measurer") was used to divide time into months, and enabled the Egyptians to create the first fixed date on a calendar, 4241 B.C. Because they divided the year into twelve months of thirty days each, they would have extra days left over which were treated as special feast days.

Religion then, in the prehistoric and early historic periods, was primarily the giving of a spirit life to nature and natural objects; this form of worship is called Animism. Even today, isolated tribal societies have been discovered practising Animism in Australia, New Zealand, Africa, Melanasia and South America.

Megalithic Monuments

Modern day archeologists have uncovered thousands of megalithic religious structures which were constructed during the Neolithic Age. Mega (large) lithic (stone) monuments are found principally in western Europe. Some of these structures are made up of stones that weigh up to eighty tons, and measure as much as sixty-one feet by sixteen feet by nine feet! Various explanations before the days of modern science were that giants or devils had put them where they were, or that they had fallen from the heavens during a struggle between good and evil. Another medieval theory was that they had been formed by lightning striking the ground.

In reality, these awesome stone formations were part

of the religious expressions of the Neolithic people who were moving westward from eastern to western Europe and up to the British Iles around 6000 to 2000 B.C.

A typical construction consisted of several large menhirs, men(stone) hir(long), placed on end with a roof or table top stone across the top. Some were covered with earth, shrubs and grass to form tombs, which are called "barrows" by the English. These tombs were evidently burial chambers and contained artifacts and skeletons. Some structures were not tombs, but were used as altars for worship. Some contain evidence of the mother goddess cult worship of the eastern Mediterranean. Some were placed in circles called cromlechs, crom (circle), lech (place). The positions of the stones in relation to the sun and the moon sometimes show that the builders had been worshippers of these heavenly bodies.

On Salisbury Plain west of London, England, is found one of the most spectacular arrangements of stones, Stonehenge. There was evidently at one time a circular bank of heaped-up earth which enclosed a ring of wooden pillars. Within the pillars, stones were strategically placed so that the altar stone and the heelstone would be in the full light of the rising sun on June 21, an important day in the calendar of a sun-worshipper. Because of its size, there are various theories about Stonehenge.

One theory is that Merlin, a legendary magician and prophet from the fifth century, was responsible. Another conclusion by Inigo Jones, who was the English king's royal architect in 1620, was that the stones were the ruins of a Roman temple. The most popular theory for a long time was that the Celtic Druids, an ancient religious sect, were responsible. Finally, it was proven to have been built about 1840 B.C. and probably has been rebuilt several times by various worshippers over the centuries, until it is now in its present state of fenced-in ruins.

It is especially mysterious that the dark blue stones that were used weigh four tons apiece and had to have come from the Prescelly Mountains in Wales, 240 miles away. The sarsen stone blocks, later used, came from the Marlborough Downs, twenty miles away, and weigh forty tons each. All this movement of stones and construction was done, of course, without benefit of modern machinery.

From the megaliths, historians have been able to draw some valuable conclusions about the many influ-

Stonehenge

ences that converged in western Europe. The herders of the Battle-Ax culture who came west out of what is now Russia brought with them the Indo- European language, the basis for most western languages today except Hungarian, Finnish and Basque. The people who came south from Scandinavia were sun-worshippers who, like the Battle-Ax people, were searching for new pastures. They met and were influenced by the westward and northward flow of Neolithic farmers who brought with them their beliefs about the spirits who watched over and influenced their crops. Sailors and merchants who sailed westward and moved northward brought the influence of their belief in the mother goddess (discussed later). Evidence indicates a mingling of these cultures that produced new and various forms of worship that were combinations of old beliefs and rituals.

An interesting contrast to the megalithic monuments is provided by a discovery in 1887 by the French archeologist, Edouard Piette. In the French Pyrenees at Azilia, he discovered hundreds of painted mini pebbles which date from the Middle Stone Age. These tiny stones were somehow used in the religion of the time and were painted with dots, crosses and parallel lines, both in patterns and in random blobs. Social scientists study clues of all sizes in order to solve the mysteries of our backgrounds.

The Realm of Mother Goddess

Because new life begins and grows within the females of all species, prehistoric and early historic worship was often directed toward a goddess as a mother figure, instead of the male principal figure that prevails in most religions today. One theory in regard to the prehistoric animal paintings in caves is that the images of hunted animals were chosen to be deliberately planted inside mountains which represented Mother Nature. There within the cave, as within the wombs of the females of any species, the animals would increase and multiply for better hunting.

The earliest statuaries of religious significance, which date from about 30,000 B.C., are female. The figures are usually depicted with exaggerated female characteristics, full breasts and pumpkin-shaped buttocks, stressing the features of fertility and nourishment. One theory about large buttocks is that they make a large lap which resembles a throne for holding and nurturing. Madonnas are sometimes pictured holding Jesus on their laps.

In the mid-1800s, an Englishman named Sir Arthur Evans uncovered the ruins of an ancient female-worshipping civilization on the island of Crete at Knossos. The culture was dated 3000 B.C. All evidence indicates that the culture consisted of peaceful, relaxed and stylishly-dressed citizens who crafted superb ceramics instead of weapons. The males wore simple straight toga-like garments while the females wore beautiful, elaborate and alluring dresses.

Here the sumptuous palace of King Minos and Queen Pariphae was excavated. Legend says that Poseidon, king

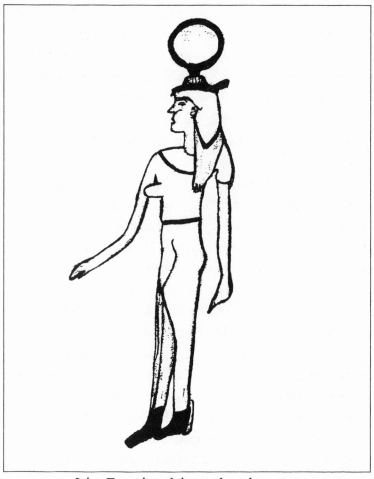

Isis, Egyptian deity and enchantress
(From the temple of Kalabsha, Lower Nubia.)

of the sea, sent this royal couple a very beautiful white bull as a gift. Because the queen fell in love with the bull, she disguised herself as a cow and eventually gave birth to the Minotaur, which was half- man, half-bull. The king confined the Minotaur within a labyrinth, to which Athens had to send tribute every nine years, in the form of fourteen noble young men and women for the bull to devour. The Greek hero, Theseus, volunteered to be one of the fourteen sacrifices, and, with the help of the Cretan princess, Ariadne, who loved him, slew the Minotaur and escaped.

This unusual culture came to an end when Crete was invaded and conquered by the warrior culture of the Greek, Mycenaeus, who worshipped the male god Zeus instead of the Earth Mother.

Mother goddess worship is evident in other early cultures. In Egypt she was called Isis; in Anatolia, Cybele; and in Syria, Astarte, to name a few. The Greeks included many goddesses in their worship, as did the Romans, and a famous sacred grove of trees dedicated to the worship of Diana, the Roman goddess of the woodland and its creatures, was located at Nem in Italy. The mysterious and highly ritualistic worship of Demeter, the Greek goddess of the harvest, and her daughter, Persephone, Queen of the Dead, at Eueusis provided a peaceful and stable religion in Attica for two thousand years until it was replaced by Christianity. Bull dancing, flowers, and beast sacrifices seemed to figure prominently in the worship rituals that honored the maternal deity.

Mother goddess figures later showed up in excavations in western Europe and it is believed that they were carried west by traders in ships from the female-worshipping cultures of the eastern Mediterranean. Some of the most famous goddess artifacts that have been found in the West are the Venus of Willendorf, found in Austria, the Venus of Menton, and the Venus of Lespugne, found in France.

A common argument in support of female worship is the quotation from the first chapter of the Book of Genesis in the Judeo-Christian Bible. It says, "So God created man *in his own image*, in the image of God He created him, *Male and Female*, He created them."

2

Ancient Historical Religions

The invention of writing by the Egyptians about five thousand years ago enabled people to keep records that give us a more detailed account of their religious customs than we have for the prehistorical period. Hieroglyphics, which means "sacred writing," were used in Egypt but were not decipherable until 1798 when a soldier of Napoleon's army discovered a particular stone tablet at Rosetta in Egypt. The irregularly-shaped stone of black basalt was 3 ft. 9 in. long by 2 ft. 4-1/2 in wide and was found on the left bank of a branch of the Nile River about thirty miles from Alexandria. The script, which was written to commemorate the ascension to the throne of

17

Ptolemy V Epiphanes in 197-6 B.C., was repeated in two forms of Egyptian script, hieroglyphics and the simpler Demotic, and also in Greek, which was familiar and made translation possible. Today the Rosetta Stone can be seen in the British Museum in London.

Translations of hieroglyphics revealed that the Egyptians were probably the first people to believe that when men died, they would have to account for how they behaved when alive. Therefore much time and energy was spent in preparation for death. Some sins could be paid for by offerings and sacrifices while alive; these gifts helped ensure a more prosperous life on Earth and a better life in the world beyond death.

Because man needed his body to travel to and enter the realm of Osiris, God of the Dead as well as of Crop Fertility, this body was mummified at death before burying it in one or more coffins within coffins. The mummifying process varied, but often consisted of soaking the body in a chemical natron solution, filling it with pitch, then wrapping it in linens that had been soaked in resins and spices.

The actual grave was large enough to hold possessions of the deceased, such as furniture, musical instruments and statues representing servants who might be needed to serve the dead person in the life beyond. Because the early graves that were dug into the sand of the rocky mountains of the west were easily robbed, the buriers piled rocks on top of the graves. These rock piles grew larger and larger until eventually they took the shape

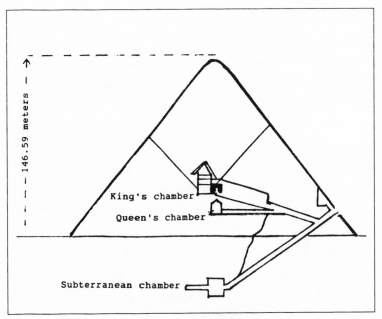

Pyramid of Khufu

of pyramids. "Pi-re-mus" means "high" in Egyptian.
The highest pyramid is that of King Khufu which was
built three thousand years ago and stands five hundred feet
high on thirteen acres of land! It took 100,000 men twenty
years to build it and is three times the size of St. Peter's
Cathedral in Rome, the world's largest Christian Church
today.

Because the Egyptian heaven, the most desirable land
in the West that was sometimes referred to as the Field of
Content or the Field of Bulrushes, was reputedly difficult
to reach because of the serpents and dragons along the
road, the dead needed to recite spells from their *Book of
the Dead.* These recitations were learned during one's

life, but copies of the text were included in the tomb just to make sure.

Egyptians believed that their good and bad deeds in life would be rewarded or punished after death. Therefore they expected that after death, they would be judged by forty-two judges, one for each different kind of sin. At this trial, Thoth, the God of Wisdom and Reckoning, weighed each person's heart on his scales which were balanced with a feather (the symbol of truth). If the heart did not balance while the person was being questioned by the judges, he was declared "false" and thrown to the "Eater of the Dead," who had the head of a crocodile, the body of a lion, and the hind of a hippopotamus. If he were declared "true," Horus led the soul to Osiris, his father, who declared him ready to enter Heaven.

The Egyptians worshipped many gods. Ra or Amon-Ra was the sun who sailed across the sky daily in his golden boat. He made warmth but he could also burn and scorch so he was respected as the most powerful god, whose symbol was a disc. Hathor, the Queen of Heaven, was symbolized by a cow. Isis, mother of Horus and wife of Osiris, was worshipped as a healer of the sick and mother goddess figure, usually pictured with the sign of the throne on her head.

Amulets were often worn by the Egyptians. Some were scarabs, large beetles, that were engraved with the name of the king or god worshipped. Some animals were sacred to them, especially the cat and the bull. These animals were sometimes embalmed and buried separately with honors.

Pharoahs, the kings of ancient Egypt, were sometimes believed to be descended from, or reincarnation of, gods. But one pharoah, Amenhatep IV, tried to change the Egyptian way by declaring that all gods were false except one, the Sun God. Because he was surrounded by priests who were more powerful than he, he was not able to carry out his ideas and, when he died, his ideas died with him and the people returned to the worship of many gods.

Mesopotamia

The word "Mesopotamia" means "the land between the two rivers," in this case the Tigris and Euphrates Rivers in Western Asia where Iraq is today. In 4000 B.C. the inhabitants were called Sumerians. They had come down from the mountains and built temples on top of the hills. These temples were unusual in that their altars were on top of the structures; from there they believed they were closer to worship their many gods. Called ziggurats, these lofty structures were pyramidal in shape and consisted of seven stages or stories, with outside staircases and a shrine at the top. Seven was an important number to these and other early people and so was used extensively in their designs.

About 2400 B.C. bands of Semitic people emigrated

from the Arabic peninsula and resettled in Mesopotamia. The name "Semitic" means "descendents of Shem, one of Noah's sons." Today we use the term to describe Jewish, Arabic, Aramaic and Ethiopic-speaking people. The most important political powers of the area were Babylonia in the south and Assyria in the north. The many gods of these early people were generally not loving gods. Marduk was the creator. Ea was the spirit of the water and he alone was considered kind, perhaps because water was so precious in this desert country. Religion did not play a major part in the life here that it did in Egypt. There was no belief in life after death. Death simply meant a descent into a dark and gloomy silence. Perhaps because there was no incentive for moral good with promise of reward, many Assyrians made robbery their chief occupation until their country was conquered in 612 B.C.

Phoenicia

Another Semitic people who believed that death consisted of going into a place of silence and becoming mute forever were the Phoenicians. They lived on the eastern shores of the Mediterranean Sea in a tiny country that was two hundred miles long and thirty-five miles wide. "Phoenicia" means "region of palms" or "fertile valley." The Phoenicians, who worked mainly as sea-going traders, worshipped many gods. Their chief god was Baal. One of the best-known Phoenicians was

Jezebel, the daughter of a Phoenician king. She married Ahab, a king of Israel, and was denounced by the Hebrew prophets who taught that there was only one God.

As businessmen, the Phoenicians considered the cuneiform (wedge-formed) writing that was invented by the Sumerians, impractical. So they took the basic wedge shapes, modified and added to them to create the first twenty-two letter alphabet. This alphabet became modified by the Greeks later, then the Romans, and the result is generally what we in the Western world use today.

Chaldea

Another significant people of this ancient area were the Chaldeans. Their worship was concentrated on the heavens and, in fact, they were responsible for the first map of the skies. They also created the Zodiac and its signs and symbols. The Zodiac, which is still used by astrologers today, is an imaginary belt in the heavens that encompasses the paths of all the planets except Pluto. Ancient Chaldean priests and contemporary astrologers have used the Zodiac and the relative positions and movements of heavenly bodies to determine and predict events on Earth. Your personal sign of the Zodiac is determined by your birthday and time. The three Magi of the Christmas story were probably Chaldeans who had seen the birth of Christ foretold in the planets and stars.

Because of many brave prophets, new religions that opposed the powerful priests began to appear in the Middle East and Asia during the sixth century, B.C.

Priests and Prophets

As primitive people banded together to worship their various gods, special persons were selected as priests to act as their intermediaries and spokesmen to the gods. These men and women took charge of a tribe's rituals and explained to the members what was required of them for spiritual health. The priests, sometimes called shamen, holy men, wakandas or orendas, were chosen because they were considered especially smart or spiritually gifted. Sometimes they simply knew more of the legends, myths and rituals of the group history, and so they could teach and lead the tribe in their practise. At times they performed mysterious tricks or magic to impress the people.

They were almost always different from other members of the tribe in some way, and they were apt to go into drug or fasting-induced spells or hallucinations. People with epileptic seizures were considered special and holy; their affliction made them eligible for the priesthood.

These holy men and women often acted as tribal doctors. They were also the ones who offered sacrifices to the gods on behalf of the group, both to make the generous gods aware of their appreciation, and to chase away or placate evil spirits.

Abuse of Power by the Priests

It became natural for the people to look up to the priests as leaders. Although some priests became greedy and corrupted by their power, the people still thought of them as necessary mediators to the gods, since they didn't think they were smart enough to speak for themselves.

After a time, unfortunately, some powerful priests began to take advantage of their trusting, dependent followers; some of them even proclaimed themselves king. Some priests insisted that elaborate blood rituals had to be performed for the gods and, as in the case of the early Brahman priests of India, they demanded money for carrying out the many animal sacrifices they said were required by their religion.

Some perceptive members started to question whether all the ceremonies and sacrifices were necessary. Certain of these questioners, called prophets, were as smart and well-informed as the priests. "Prophet" means "one who speaks on behalf of another." Many of the early prophets came from the Middle East and traveled around from tribe to tribe, teaching and talking to people. They could do this pretty easily because all the Middle Eastern languages at that time were similar. Not very much is known about the private lives of these speakers, but we do know that they all started teaching people because they had visions that God or angels told them to do so.

Elijah, an early Hebrew prophet, was a shepherd of great energy who came from the desert and preached that Jehovah was, indeed, the God of Israel. He reminded the Jews to listen to Him and to obey His commandments. He especially preached against the priests of "false" gods like Baal, the god of the Phoenician princess, Jezebel, who married Ahab, king of Israel in the ninth century before Christ.

Amos, the prophet who appeared about one hundred years later, emphasized that Jehovah was the God of all the people, not just a select group. He also taught that this God required people to serve Him and to be responsible for themselves and for each other.

Isaiah was a calm and steadfast man of vision who preached against petty meanness. He encouraged people to act with the honor, goodness and courage of which they were capable, especially during battles, as when the Assyrian army was advancing toward Jerusalem and instilling fear into the hearts of the people.

Jeremiah was a different king of prophet. He was basically a shy, sad, sensitive and lonely man who became depressed and sick-at-heart when people would not listen to his pleas for moral amendment. He was not popular because he denounced his neighbors, championed causes that were unpopular in the seventh century before Christ, and often predicted doom and gloom. But he was extremely courageous in standing up for what he believed and in doing what God had called on him to do.

Because of these and the many other brave prophets that we shall look at, new religions that opposed the powerful priests began to appear in the Middle East and Asia during the sixth century, B.C. In fact, seven popular religions appeared or grew much more vital within fifty years of that century, and these seven have endured until today. One of the seven religions that became more organized and stronger at that time, although its roots had evolved much earlier, was Judaism.

Judaism

Monotheism means "believing in one god." Judaism is the oldest monotheistic religion. According to their tradition, the Jews' religious experience began when God spoke to Abraham of Ur in the lower Mesopotamian Valley, promising him that if Abraham would leave Ur and go to the land of Canaan (Israel today), he would have children, find happiness, and act as intermediary for "all the families of the Earth."

When the Jews moved into the land of Goshen, which was in Egypt on the eastern Nile River delta, they generally lived as nomadic herders. In 1700-1600 B.C., invaders from the east called Hyksos, meaning "foreign

rulers'' in Egyptian, conquered Egypt. They employed
some of the Jews as their civil servants, using them to act
as their tax collectors. These tax collectors were not
popular with the people, and when the Hyksos eventually
overthrown by the Egyptians, the Jews became slaves to
the succeeding Egyptian rulers.

Exodus

About 1500 B.C., God spoke to the prophet, Moses,
and instructed him to lead the Jewish slaves of the Egyptians out of bondage to the land of Israel. This journey,
which is described in the Book of Exodus in the Bible's
Old Testament, was very long and difficult. According to
legend, God helped the Jews along the way. One story
relates that when they were crossing the Red Sea, the
wind from the east blew so strongly that it kept the water
in their path shallow and fordable. When however, the
pursuing chariots of the pharaoh's army entered the sea
path, the wind suddenly died and caused the Egyptians to
drown..

On another part of the journey, it is said that ''the
Lord went before them by day in a pillar of cloud to lead
them the way; and by night in a pillar of fire to give
them light; to go by day and night.'' This story relates
well to the customs of the desert travelers of that time.
The leader of a group or caravan such as theirs would
carry a long pole on top of which there would be a brazier
full of smoky coals and glowing embers. The smoke

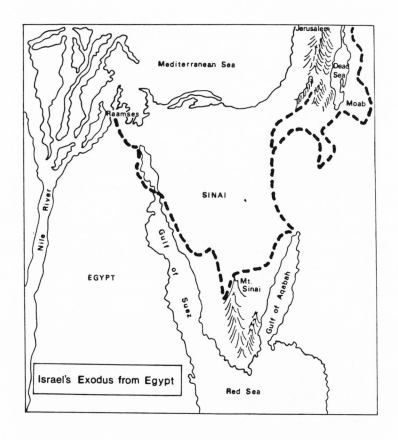

Israel's Exodus from Egypt

would make "a pillar of cloud" and the embers "a pillar of fire" that would make the carrier more visible to his followers.

At a place called Mount Sinai, God was supposed to have given to Moses the Ten Commandments, the rules by which people were instructed to live. These Ten Commandments form the basis for Judaism and also for Christianity which followed. In Judaism, the commandments are called the Law of Moses. When the prophet asked God his name, God said, "I Am That I Am." When this was written in Hebrew, "I Am" became YHWH and God became known to the Hebrews as Yahweh. Other names for God in Jewish scriptures are Elohim and Adonay.

Hebrew Texts

The Old Testament of the Bible (meaning "book") is a collection of stories describing what happened to the Jewish people from the time of the creation of the world by God until the time preceding the birth of Jesus Christ. First written in Hebrew, it was later translated into Greek, Roman, and then into almost all other languages of the world.

The first five books of the Bible are sometimes referred to as the Pentateuch or the Torah. "Torah" means "divine instruction" and it is also used as a specific reference to a sacred parchment scroll which contains the Law of Moses. It explains Jewish law and contains 613 rules for daily living. Men who copy these holy scrolls are called Sofers who lead moral and exemplary lives. Copies of the Torah are kept in the Ark of every synagogue. The Ark is a repository in or near the wall of the temple. When copies of sacred writings are worn out, they are reverently buried in a grave.

The Diaspora

In the sixth century B.C., when the Jews were living in Canaan (roughly what is now Palestine), the Babylonian king, Nebuchadrezzar II, destroyed the main city of Jerusalem with his army and took the Jews and everyone else prisoner to Babylon. Then Cyrus, the powerful Persian king, captured Babylon and allowed the Jews to return to Jerusalem, rebuild their temple, and practice their own faith once again. In A.D. 70, Jerusalem was razed again, this time by the Romans who came to put down a Jewish rebellion against their rule. Many Jews left at that time to settle outside of Palestine; this scattering of the Jews is called the Diaspora. Today in Jerusalem there is a Wailing Wall, so called because it is a wall of the temple that was left standing and is where Jews may go to pray and mourn the destruction of their temple and Jerusalem.

Zionism

Zionism is an important concept of Judaism. It is the name of the movement whose purpose has always been to return the Jews to Palestine where they feel they belong, and specifically to Jerusalem. Begun about 1917 and spearheaded by Dr. Chaim Weizman, Zionism has always stressed the need for Jews to have their homeland and not be scattered throughout the world. After years of occupation by various conquering armies, the desired homeland of Judaism came to be focused upon by the United Nations. In 1947, members of the U.N. tried to settle the problem by voting to partition Palestine into Jewish Israel and Arabic Jordan. In 1948 the settlement was sealed and the state of Israel, with about 10,000 square miles of land, was established.

Although much Judaic worship is done at home, Jews hold regular services and practise rituals in their temples, called synagogues. In lieu of priests, they have rabbis who are the teachers of Judaism. One of the early rabbis was Hillel, who taught in the first century, B.C. that Jews should live by the Golden Rule: you should treat others as you would like them to treat you. "What is hateful to thee, do not unto thy fellowman; this is the whole Law. The rest is but commentary." This lesson of Hillel is found in many other religions, such as Christianity, Confucianism, Jainism and Buddhism.

Teaching was done orally until the second century A.D. when the councils of rabbis systematically defined the Mishnah, the writings of instruction. The Mishnah formed the basis for the Talmud. Since then, various writings of learned Jews have been added to these rules for civil and canonical conduct.

Religion is a very important part of a Jewish person's life. Also called Hebrews, meaning "dwellers on the other side," they believe that there is one God who gives men free will, rewards goodness, and punishes evil. They believe in a judgment time for everyone when he must answer for his behavior in life, and in a Messiah who will come to Earth to rescue them from evil.

There are several categories of Jews. Orthodox Jews live strictly according to the social, religious and dietary rules as defined in the Torah. Reform Jews are liberal and progressive; they encourage changes in the religion to reflect changes in society, while not losing the basic spiritual, ethical and ceremonial aspects of the faith. Conservative Jews are cautious about radical changes and stress a middle-of-the-road attitude of study and learning from knowing and interpreting the unique history of Israel. Finally, Hasidic Jews are an ultra orthodox pietistical group who, since the 18th century, have been rigidly committed to their own interpretation of the Torah laws. They tend not to mingle with people from other religions, and are distinguished by the unique long curls worn by the males of the sect.

When a Hebrew is twelve or thirteen years old, he takes part in a ceremony called Bar Mitzvah (son of duty) for boys and Bas Mitzvah for girls. In this important ritual, children of Jewish parents take responsibility for their own religious lives.

Orthodox Jews have strict dietary laws. They may eat only food which is Kosher, that is, it is fit and clean according to their particular specifications and has been blessed by a rabbi. The Jewish Sabbath begins on Friday at sundown with a special candlelit meal at home called the Seder, at which certain foods must be eaten. No work can be done on the Sabbath and Jews attend a worship service in the synagogue. This attendance is mandatory for men, while women are allowed to attend also. At the entrance to the synagogue, a Jew purifies his hands with water. This purification ritual is found in many other religions, such as Shintoism and Catholic Christianity. Then a Jew will touch his lips to the scriptures set near the entrance. There are readings from the Bible, a sermon by the rabbi, singing, alms-giving and confession, all similar to what is done in Christian church services. The Sabbath ends at sundown on Saturday with a home service that includes wine and sweet spices.

Judaism celebrates many holy days during the year. The Hebrew calendar starts with the date 3761 B.C. and the Jewish New Year occurs in September. Called Rosh Hashanah, it is a day of thoughtful meditation and resolution to do better.

Yom Kippur comes ten days after Rosh Hashanah and is the Day of Atonement. It is spent as a day of rest, repentance and reconciliation with God. Hanukkah is an eight-day celebration in late November or early December. It commemorates the Maccabean victory of the Jews over the Greeks in the second century B.C.. The Maccabees were a Jewish family who led the revolt against Hellenistic rule.

Some other holidays are: Purim in February or March, the Festival of Deliverance; Shabuoth, fifty days after Passover, celebrating the first fruits of harvest time; and Sukkoth, the most important harvest festival. Passover is probably the most meaningful of Jewish festivals. "Pazah" means "to skip over" in Hebrew and Passover is celebrated in memory of the story in which the "angel of death" passed over and spared the houses of the Jews in Egypt that had been marked with the blood of a lamb. The marking was done because Moses had repeated to the Jews God's warning to him, that because the Pharaoh would not release the Jews from slavery, one midnight God would cause a plague of death to come to all first-born children in the land of Egypt. This plague would affect all families from royalty to animals, except those living in houses marked by the lambs' blood. The Feast of Passover commemorates this event.

Today there are more than seventeen million Jews, living mostly in Israel and the United States, but there are Jewish communities in almost all countries of the world.

If the red slayer thinks he slays,
And if the slain thinks he is slain,
He knoweth not my subtle ways,
I turn and pass and turn again.

Hinduism

During the time of the Jewish exodus from Egypt, a different culture was developing in India. When a tall, fair-skinned people from southeastern Europe called Aryans (meaning "noble") invaded the lands of southern Asia, they found there a darker-skinned people. Living together, these two peoples developed a way of life that is called Hinduism. "Hindu" means "Indian" in the Persian language. Today there are 689,205,100 Hindus, living mostly in India, but also in Myanmar, Sri Lanka, Thailand, Melanesia, Vietnam, South Africa and in other areas of the world. Hinduism is different in that it had no particular prophet or founder and is rather a way of life based on certain beliefs that have evolved in ways that varied from place to place. Although the ancient Aryans brought with them the practise of sacrificing to the gods of nature, Hindus came to believe that all life is sacred and so sacrifice is wrong. They say that one who cannot give life has no right to take it away. They do not kill any living creature: insect, animal, bird or human; this practise is called "ahimsa." A famous non-Hindu who believed in ahimsa was Dr. Albert Schweitzer of Gabon in twentieth-century Africa. Hindus do not eat meat, and they consider cows especially sacred, although no one seems to know why. Cows are often seen walking freely along the busy streets of Indian cities today.

Rivers are also sacred since they bring life to the land. Bathing in the Ganges River is a ritual which brings blessings to the bather, and scattering the ashes of the cremated dead on the river's surface is done for the same reason.

Hindu expectations of after-death experience are based on reincarnation, the rebirth of a human soul in a new body. Souls of those who lead wicked lives are reborn as animals or insects, while the souls of the good are elevated in status the next time around. A person's life, therefore, is not accidental or meaningless, but is a working out of his previous life and the predetermining of his future one. The time period of your life and your actions therein are called your "karma." Your goal should be to live a moral life doing your duty ("dharma") so well that eventually you can be released from transmigration, the cycle of death and rebirth, and reach "moksha," which is eternal peace and unity with Brahma. Brahma is the supreme neutral, peaceful and impersonal god who is the unknowable cosmic force of nature. He is called the World Soul and is depicted with four heads to show that he is all-seeing and all-knowing.

Brahma is also the Creator in the Hindu Trinity, along with Vishnu, the Preserver, and Shiva, the Destroyer. Besides the Trinity, there are a myriad of lesser deities. A Hindu of any class can choose to worship the gods or goddesses that best suit his particular needs. In temples and in shrines at home, Hindus offer prayers ("mantras"), incense, food and flowers to the gods. Sarasvati, goddess of learning, and Shakti, goddess of

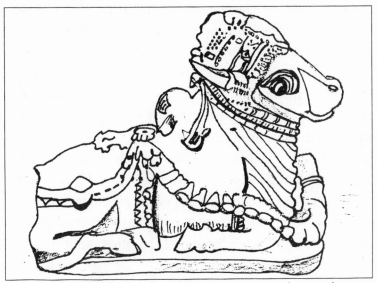

Nandi - The Hindu god Shiva's mount and sometimes Shiva's animal form.

universal energy, are two very popular goddesses. Ganesh, the elephant god, symbolizes wisdom, prudence, and good luck. Hanuman, the monkey god, is supposed to have once leaped across the water between mainland India and Sri Lanka, a distance of one hundred miles, in one great bound!

The Sacred Thread

Like Jewish young people, Hindus are initiated into their faith when they are about twelve or thirteen years old. The ceremony of taking the "Sacred Thread" takes place in the home in the presence of a priest and relatives. After his head is shaved, the candidate sits with his father before a holy fire while the priest pierces his ears with a needle to indicate his readiness to take in the holy spirit, then he gives him a sacred thread. The young person fixes his eyes on the thread and meditates about his relationship to Brahma, while the priest chants a mantra. The person and his/her father then reverently chant, "Om," a mystical Hindu word that signifies Brahma. Next, the person is left in a dark and silent room for three days. He meditates on his new relationship with his god until, after three days of fasting, his mother brings him some food, usually rice and vegetables. That is the end of the ritual, after which there is a family celebration.

Sacred Writings

Hindus learn how to live morally by studying ancient writings, especially the four holy Vedas. Supposedly conceived by Brahman himself and written down by holy men in the period from 1500 to 800 BC., the *Rig Veda* is made up of one thousand plus hymns to gods. The *Sam Veda* is a book of revelation, the *Yajur Veda* consists of hymns and mantras, and the *Artharva Veda* is a book of charms and incantations. Other important texts are the *Upanishads* and the *Sutras.* There are also some long epic poems that teach Hindus how to find the meaning and purpose of life. "The Ramayana" and "The Mahabarata" are two of these.

"The Mahabarata" consists of 220,000 lines and is the longest epic poem in the world. In it, "The Bhagavad Gita" relates a dialogue between the god, Krishna, and the warrior, Arjuna, in which it is revealed how to reach moksha by knowledge through meditation. This knowledge leads to goodness from following moral rules, having courage, and seeking the path of love.

Besides the priests of Hinduism, there are "sadhus," holy men who live very humbly and spend their lives teaching others how to live morally. One very special Hindu leader was Mohandas Ghandi, a political leader and lawyer who stressed the importance of ahimsa, of living peacefully, of loving and respecting people of other cultures and religions. He was assassinated by a radical Hindu in 1948, leaving behind all of his possessions: a rice bowl, a Bible, his simple garment and his eyeglasses.

Tolerance is important to Hinduism. Believing that "all roads that lead to God are good," they admire and respect holy men and prophets of all faiths. They send out no missionaries, and they do not try to convert others to their faith.

Yoga in Hinduism

Yoga is a discipline often practised by Hindus who are trying to increase in knowledge. A yogi helps disciples to develop spiritually by promoting pure thought, pure actions, pure breathing, pure exercises and pure self-awareness. Basically divided into two parts, "Hatha" or exercise and "Rajah" or meditation, this discipline involves concentration that leads to self-controlled deep meditation. Often practised while in a particular position like a "lotus" posture or a head stand, the yogi may also be chanting or humming. This concentration brings total relaxation and a loss of self as one is absorbed into a sense of being part of a greater whole. Yoga is practised all over the world by people who want to relax while developing their psychic powers within a deeper understanding of themselves and their lives. This process is sometimes called transcendental meditation (spiritual thinking).

"The Bhagavad Gita" epitomizes the discipline of yoga in this way:

"Having mastered the body through the Yogic

teachings so that it becomes a fit habitation for the soul; having the senses, emotions and mind under control, the wise person discards the wornout sheaths of desire, fear and confusion and passes into the state of enlightenment and freedom.''

Although most worship is done at home before shrines to their particular gods, Hindus have beautiful temples where they hold festivals of music, dancing and processions to honor their gods. They also hold classes there, in which people can learn from the sacred texts or a yogi teacher.

A Hindu wedding is a very special event. In front of a holy fire in the temple, the groom places vermillion on the forehead of the bride and clasps an iron bracelet on her wrist. The coupld are usually not very well known to each other, since they are traditionally chosen by their parents. Hindus say, ''Marriage should be the beginning, not the end, of romance.'' Joining hands, the couple say, ''I take hold of your hand for good fortune so that, with you, I may attain old age. I am the words and you are the melody; I am the melody and you are the words.''

The Caste System

When you are born a Hindu, you are automatically a member of the social class, or caste, to which your parents belong. Caste is explained by a legend about the origin of man and is defended as fair because it is part of the wheel of justice (karma) as set in motion by Brahma.

According to the ancient story, a god named Perusa told Brahma he would sacrifice himself so man could be created. Brahma agreed and when Perusa was sacrificed on the altar of heaven, a miracle occurred. Out of Perus's mouth, Brahman priests were created. Out of his arms, Ksatriyas warriors came. From his thighs, Vaisyas businessmen Hindus emerged, and from his feet were created the Sudras laborers.

Historically, what actually happened was this:

In Sanskrit the word for caste is "varna" which means "color." The light-skinned Aryans considered themselves superior to the dark-skinned Indus inhabitants and encouraged separation of the people into classes. These classes are sometimes privileged like the Brahmins' caste or very underprivileged like the Untouchables' caste. Your caste determines whom you can marry and what occupations you can follow. The only way you can improve your caste is to die and be reborn into another one. Although the Indian government has outlawed this caste system, it still exists in parts of India.

When a Hindu dies, his body is colorfully shrouded and cremated on a funeral pyre on the banks of a river. Then the ashes are scattered into the river. A former custom required that widows throw themselves into the funeral fire of their deceased husbands; this custom of "suttee" is no longer followed.

The American poet and philosopher, Ralph Waldo Emerson, had great respect for Hinduism although he was

a practising Christian himself. In his nineteenth century
poem, "Brahma," he epitomized the faith when he wrote:

> *"If the red slayer thinks he slays,*
> *And if the slain thinks he is slain,*
> *He knoweth not my subtle ways,*
> *I turn and pass and turn again."*

*"The foundation of this religion
is a consistent and pervasive reverence
for all life. "*

The Jains

During the sixth century, B.C., some Hindus of India, many of whom were of Aryan background, rejected much of what they were being taught by the priests and formed the nucleus of a new religious group called the Jains. A Hindu prince named Nataputta Vardhamana, who was also called Lord Mahavira (the Great Hero), was their leader. He was born the son of the King of Mogadah in northern India in 600 B.C. Legend tells that when a small boy, he was playing one day with friends in the palace garden. Suddenly a bull elephant came charging into the garden. While the other children ran, the prince stood his ground, caught the elephant's trunk, climbed onto his back, and drove him back to the royal stables to be chained. Since that incident, he was called the Lord Mahavira.

At the age of twelve, Mahavira took the Sacred Thread and began to study Hinduism with the priests. From the very beginning, he questioned the wisdom of some of Hinduism's basic beliefs. At nineteen, he married happily and lived in the palace with his wife for ten contented years.

Then it happened that he was deeply affected by the voluntary deaths of his parents, the king and queen, who starved themselves in order to die a "holy" death. Following this event, he took a vow to remain silent for twelve years. He began to travel, dressed as a commoner, observing and meditating on what he saw. He reached some conclusions about what was wrong with Hinduism and about the secrets of leading a moral life. After twelve years of silence, he began to teach and attract followers. These disciples were mostly wealthy men like himself who also gave up their possessions to follow his example.

These first Jains rejected all the gods, prayers and the caste system of the Hindus. They believed that a person is alone responsible for his salvation; he creates his own individual karma according to his own perceptions. Only when a person reaches Nirvana (Moksha) can he be expected to understand everything. A popular Jain parable illustrates this belief:

There are six blind men who are asked to touch and describe an elephant. The man who takes hold of the tail says that an elephant must be something like a rope, long and thin. The man who seizes the trunk describes the elephant as looking like a snake. The one who takes part of a leg in his hand says that the animal is definitely shaped like a tree trunk, and the other three men have their own particular distorted perceptions, depending on which part of the animal they have touched. The idea, of course, is to illustrate how limited our perceptions are and how faulty our subjective conclusions.

The Jains believe that Mahavira was the twenty-fourth and last of a line of Jains (conquerors) that really began trillions of years ago with a Jain named Adinath. This belief is based on myth and has no written history. The sacred book of Jainism is *the Agamas* which means "precepts" and contains the sermons of Mahavira.

The Code of Ahimsa

The foundation of this religion is a consistent and pervasive reverence for all life. Jains adhere strictly to the code of ahimsa, are committed to non-violence, and are strict vegetarians. Along with abstinence from meat of all kinds, they will not cut trees nor farm the land because of plants and animals that could be harmed by plowing and chemicals. Trees, fire, water, vegetables, all have souls, and human souls that are reincarnated can return in any other living form, say as a beet or an onion! Jains will not work with metal or wood because these substances may

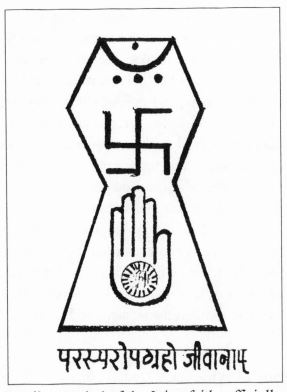

परस्परोपग्रहो जीवानाम्

Jaina Pratika: symbol of the Jaina faith, officially adoped in 1975. The palm of the hand bears the word ahimsa; the swastika topped by three dots and the crescent represent the four distinies, the threefold path, and the abode of the liberated souls, respectively; the slogan below the figure of loka-akasa calls for the mutual assistance of all beings.''

suffer pain in the process. So in order to earn a living, they have avoided dealing in living organisms by becoming tradesmen, bankers and other kinds of businessmen. Because they are involved in business, most Jains live in large cities and have prospered there.

In rituals of birth, marriage and death, Jains follow regular Hindu customs; otherwise they stress giving up desire for, and attachment to, worldly possessions. They advocate honesty, truthfulness, humility and chastity.

Some members become ascetics, who have no possessions except enough clothing to cover themselves. They shave off their hair, keep no home, endure self-torture, and form no loving attachments to other persons. A Jain ascetic is apt to be pictured sleeping on a bed of nails, detached from everyone and everything in the world.

It is central to Jain belief that effort, knowledge and discipline are the ways you can control your karma. Selfish, cruel or careless actions, all sins, make your soul heavy. A soul that is heavy sinks, even as far as the seven hells that lie below. Good deeds, on the other hand, lighten the soul, and when it is light enough, it can float upward through the twenty-six heavens and ultimately to the top of the universe and Nirvana. A Jain woman has an added burden in that she cannot hope to reach Nirvana as a woman. She must first be reborn as a man in order to qualify!

From a very small beginning 2600 years ago, Jainism has grown to include 3,581,500 members in India, mostly living in and around cities. Although there were originally no prayers nor temples in which to pray, there are today over 40,000 Jain temples, including some of the most beautiful buildings of the world. Jains also maintain homes for elderly cows and hospitals for animals, birds and even insects.

The Sikh's goal is to reach a sense of union with God. Nirvana is described as the "cessation of individual consciousness caused by the blending of the light of the soul with the light of God."

The Sikhs

In the northwestern part of the Indian-Pakistani subcontinent, there is a region with five rivers called the Punjab, which means "five waters." The Punjab, gateway to the Orient since the thirteenth century travels of Marco Polo, is an area that has been politically invaded and historically dominated by various groups for centuries.

From the eighth to the fifteenth centuries A.D., the Hindus that lived there were overrun by invading Muslims from the West. Because of the many problems and abuses arising from conflicting religious beliefs and practises, a Hindu named Nanak founded the compromise religion of Sikhism in the fifteenth century. "Sikh" is a Sanskrit word meaning "disciple." Nanak became the first guru of the Sikhs. "Guru" means "teach" and he was the primary teacher, first of ten in all. To a Sikh, God is the most important guru.

Nanak was born A.D. 1469 in a small village in what is now West Pakistan. Even as a child, he was very concerned with matters of the spirit, although he led an average life until the age of thirty. At that time he began to travel about, preaching compromises between the religions of Hinduism and Islam, two very different ways of worship. (See Chapters 5 and 16.) His lessons that taught acceptance of all people for redemption and his simplifying of religious practises were drastic changes for Hindus used to the complicated and exclusive worship of idols and images of many gods.

Along with his rejection of polytheism, he strongly opposed the caste system. When asked why the Hindu people had to suffer so much, he replied that they were conquerable because they must have lost their virtue, and that only by recovering truth and goodness could they hope for salvation. This recovery was possible, he taught, by "prasada" (grace) from "rhakti" (loving adoration of God). This grace was open to all people of all classes, even women and members of low classes such as the previously unredeemable Untouchables. In his chosen role of peacemaker, he became loved by both Hindus and Moslems.

Nanak was critical of hypocrisy and wealth acquired at the expense of others. In an incident that illustrates his beliefs, it is said that he was once invited to attend a lavish dinner at the home of a very rich Muslim named Malik Bhago. He declined the invitation in order to share a simple meal with some poor friends. When asked by Bhago why he did this, he responded by taking some bread from each table. In his left hand, he squeezed the bread from the table of the rich man until out came drops of blood. In his right hand he squeezed the bread from the poor man's table until out came drops of milk.

This beloved and respected guru preached universal brotherhood, equality, and love for everyone. He urged self-discipline in a body and mind that were kept healthy and sound.

Nanak's Successors

His chosen succeeding guru, Angad, was the disciple who invented the Punjabi language and built the first Sikh temples, called "gurdwaras", as places for teaching his lessons. Amardas, the third guru, was also a disciple. After his appointing of Ramdas, his son-in-law, as his successor, the rest of the ten gurus who followed came from one family. Arjan, the fifth guru, was falsely accused of tax evasion and executed by the Mughal Emperor, Jahangir, who feared Arjan's influence with the people.

Sikh Militarism

The unfair execution of Arjan changed the Sikhs from a pacifist group to a military sect. They began to train assiduously and became respected for their skills as soldiers. Gobind Singh, the tenth and final guru, polished the Sikh military machine when he asked for volunteers to form the elite Khalsa ("the pure").

Members of Khalsa received new names, all with "Singh" ("lion") for a suffix. They swore an oath to the five K's: Keah - wearing long hair; Kangha - a comb in their hair; Kachha - soldier's shorts; Kara - a steel bangle on the right wrist; Kirpan - a saber. Their words of initiation were, "The Khalsa are the chosen of God, victory be to God."

Since Gobind Singh lost all four of his sons in his lifetime, he put an end to the guru succession in 1708, stating that teaching would be done henceforth from their holy book, *The Granth Sahib*. A Hindu ascetic disciple, Banda Singh Bahadur, carried on the work of Gobind Singh when he died, fighting the tyranny of the Muslim rulers. Besides the savage persecution of their members by the Muslims, they suffered great losses at the hands of invading Afghans. Their temples were destroyed and, in one battle with them, over 30,000 Sikhs were killed!

In spite of these setbacks, the Sikhs multiplied and prospered during this difficult period because of the remarkable leadership of Kapur Singh and Jassa Singh Ahluwalia, who divided the Sikhs into twelve effective misls (militias). They had considerable success deposing Muslim tyrants, but then, unfortunately, they began to fight each other. Finally, Ranjit Singh of Sukarchakia Misl absorbed all the units and unified them once again. He ruled for about forty years, from 1799 until 1840, but at the time of his death, no one was able to succeed him and make it work.

The British, who had occupied India by then, annexed the Punjab to British India after the Sikh Wars from 1845 to 1849. During the two World Wars, the Sikhs fought as respected soldiers on the side of the British.

When the British relinquished power in India, the country was partitioned and most of the Sikh population occupied the Punjab. Today, that is where most of the world's 17,735,100 Sikhs live, but there are also Sikhs in Great Britain, the United States, Canada, Thailand, Myanmar, Singapore and Hong Kong.

Sikhism teaches that there is one God who is indestructible and who can pardon sins. Members worship no idols nor images. Prayer, especially the repetition of the name of God, is extremely important, and assists the soul to pass through stages of transmigration until it reaches Nirvana, union with God.

There are no religious rites and no priests. Any person of either sex can lead a religious group in the study or recitation of selections from *The Granth Sahib*, which contains the teachings of Nanak and the other gurus. In it are contained 5894 hymns on 1439 pages.

Yoga is encouraged, as are all disciplines that are

good for the body and mind. Alcohol and tobacco are forbidden as injurious to the mind and body. Cremation is practised at death.

Young Sikhs take part in an initiation ceremony of the Five K's at puberty. The boys take "Singh" as an additional name; the girls take the name "Kaur."

The daily obligations of a Sikh are few. They are supposed to bathe early and to recite five prayers. Encouraged are habits of honesty, humility, sharing of wealth and happiness, non-violence and peaceful coexistence.

Anyone may attend a Sikh service in a temple. It is a place that is used as a community center and as a place of study of the *Guru Granth,* for music, lectures and singing of hymns. The birth of a child is celebrated by taking him to the gurdwara (house of God) and distributing sweets to all present.

Marriage is encouraged and recognized as the ideal within the normal life of society. Anyone can perform a marriage in the temple. The bride wears a red or pink tunic and trousers called "shalwar-kameez" and there are recitations from the holy book.

Sikh men traditionally wear a fifteen-foot length of cloth, usually white, wrapped around the head turbanwise. It is traditional for a male to assume this turban when he becomes the head of a family, for it is the guru symbol of authority.

There have been some modifications in the dress code of the Five K's code, i.e. the saber or sword is now apt to be a piece of metal imbedded within the required comb. Men continue to let their hair and beards grow long however. Their clothing is usually white, both men and women's, and often consists of simply-styled shirts and tunics.

The Sikh's goal is to reach a sense of union with God. He tries to overcome the selfishness, pride and love of material things that keep people alienated from God. This union, or Nirvana, is described as the "cessation of individual consciousness caused by the blending of the light of the soul with the light of God."

Nanak left no written lessons, but he did leave some songs. One, called "Nirvana," epitomizes his religion:

> *"As water blends with water,*
> *When two streams their waves unite,*
> *The light of human life doth blend*
> *With God's celestial light.*
> *No transmigrations then await*
> *The weary human soul;*
> *It hath attained its resting place,*
> *Its peaceful crowning goal."*

Life on Earth is basically a struggle between good and evil.

The Parsees

Another religious group that coexists with the Indian Hindus today are the 2,000,000 Parsees (meaning "Persians") who live mostly in and around the city of Bombay. Although comparatively few in number, members of this religion form an important part of the Indian culture. They are considered the best-educated, most cultured, most industrious and charitable people of the land.

These Parsees are descendants of the followers of Zoroaster of Persia (now Iran) who, in the seventh century B.C., taught that there was one god, Ahura-Mazdah, who is the creator and guardian of mankind. Because of this belief, the Parsees in Persia eventually were forced to leave there and resettle in India to escape the persecution of invading Muslims.

Before Zoroaster, the Persian farmers and herders worshipped many gods of nature called "daivas." There were also gods of clan, family and society. Images and idols of gold and silver were made and worshipped in great temples run by priests. These priests practised magic to influence the people and the gods, and were called "magi." Some of them became very rich and powerful, and began to think of themselves as better than the rest of the Persian people. Then along came Zoroaster.

Not much is known about Zoroaster's early life, but we do know that he was born in 660 B.C. and that he was a different and special boy. He studied religion, farming and healing. As a child and as a young man, he always ministered to those wounded, sick or needy people that he saw were suffering pain or sorrow. Although normally and happily married to the beautiful Havovee, he was not content, so at the age of thirty he withdrew from society and lived alone in the forest. There he sought to understand the conflict between good and evil in the world and how it could be resolved. The answer came to him in a series of dreams and visions from God, (Ahura-Mazdah) and he returned to teach people what he had learned. It was long after his death in the years around 900 A.D. that the followers of his teaching left Persia and resettled in India.

Good vs Evil

Parsees believe that life on Earth is basically a struggle between good and evil. Ahura-Mazda is opposed by Ahriman, the Prince of Darkness. Mazda's six holy spirits are opposed by demon spirits. By good spirits, Zoroaster did not mean angels with wings and haloes. He meant instead the six characteristics of man that help him to be and do good: good mind, good order, wisdom, piety, well-being and immortality. Man, in his desire to do what is right, has to ask for help in resisting evil by prayers to Mazda and the six good spirits. Knowledge is particularly important in developing an understanding of what is good and what is evil. After the understanding is reached, man makes the choice of following good or evil, knowing that his life and character will be judged when he dies.

In ancient practise, Zoroastrians were apt to use astrology, alchemy, occultism and any magic they felt would help guide them toward goodness. Although they believe that Christian teaching is good, their main source of help is Zoroaster, whose words are in their sacred book, *The Avesta*. The original *Zend-Avesta* was supposed to have been written in gold letters on 12,000 ox hides. This original copy doesn't exist today, having been destroyed by war.

To be truly good, a Parsee must be kind to all: people, animals, the Earth, and even in his thoughts. Parsees are among the happiest people in India; crime and divorce are extremely rare among them. In a land where all life is considered sacred, the Parsees are especially known for their love of animals. According to Friedrich Nietzsche in his book, *Thus Spake Zarathustra* (Zoroaster), the prophet had spoken with tender concern for all creatures, particularly the dog whom he regarded as man's companion and helper.

The Ceremony of Navajot

When a Parsee is nine years old, he goes through a ceremony called Navajot, in which he becomes a member of the responsible adult community. Just before the ceremony, he discards his child costume, the sacklike "zabhalan." As an adult Parsee, he will assume wearing a white cotton shirt which is tied with a lambswool cord. This cord will be untied and retied five times daily while prayers to Mazda are said.

To prepare for Navajot, a Parsee child attends classes that are strictly taught by bearded priests out of doors in the scorching sunshine. The priests stand over him with a stick while he recites prayers and other recitations from *The Avesta*, loudly and necessarily perfectly.

On the day of Navajot, all of his friends and relatives come to the candidate's house early to attend the long and solemn ceremony. During the ritual, he must remember to look to the East always and never to the North which is the stronghold of evil magnetic forces that will cloud the mind and disturb the chanting of the priests. During the prayers and recitations done by both the priests and the communicant, he drinks and is anointed with "nirangdeen," the sanctified urine of a great white holy bull who is kept tethered at the temple. This is done to wish him the powers of procreation, for marriage and children are very important to the Parsees.

Eventually his mother brings him a tray on which there is rice, a coconut, an egg and a pitcher of water. She whirls the egg and coconut three times over his head, then breaks them to see if the egg is rotten or the coconut discolored, omens of bad luck. Then he is escorted to a white cloth-covered dais where a sandlewood fire burns and where trays of food and gifts wait for him. Twelve priests gather around him and chant with him as he is dressed in the sacred shirt with the belt of lambswool. In this way he assumes responsibility for his own spiritual life.

Parsee Marriage

When a Parsee matures, he is encouraged to marry within his faith and to have children. *The Avesta* says, "He that hath a wife is far above him that liveth in continence; he that maintaineth a household is far above him that hath none; he that hath children is far above him that hath no child." Parsees choose their own marital partners, sometimes with the help of their parents. First cousins are allowed to marry, and Parsees are tolerant of women who become pregnant before marriage.

A Parsee wedding is held in a garden in which a platform has been erected and beautifully decorated. Two white-robed priests lead the bride and groom to two chairs on the platform, separated by a white curtain. A priest questions them about loving and honoring each other, while their friends and relatives look on. Then they join hands under the curtain while the priest winds a string around their hands seven times. Then he winds the string around their chairs seven times also. Seven is a propitious number to the Persians. There are seven virtues, seven deadly sins, seven archangels with God, and some authorities say there are also seven good and evil spirits that do battle for the souls of men.

After the winding, the priest knots the ends of the string in the couple's hands while chanting passages from *The Avesta* about the importance of faith in their lives for their future life together. He removes the curtain that separates them, explaining that the bound hands symbolize their spiritual union, and the bound chairs symbolize religion binding them to their mutual home. Then he removes the thread. Now the bride and groom toss rice at each other as a sign of a fruitful life together. Musicians play and the priest sermonizes about attitudes necessary for a happy marriage. After more prayers, there are gifts and a feast for all.

Fire: a Sacred Symbol

Fire is the most important sacred symbol of the Parsee faith. The source of the original flame was a lightning bolt that was sent to Earth by Ahura-Mazda. Ancient Persians took some of the sparks from this bolt to start a fire which is supposed to have been kept burning ever since. In some Parsi temples, it is known that fires have been burning continually for at least a thousand years! Members who come to the temple to pray bring sandlewood offerings for the fire which they are not allowed to see, and which is fed only by the white-robed priests. In our culture today, we have light bulbs and cars with the trade name of "Mazda,"a commercial distortion of a sacred name.

Because fire is holy to them, Parsees do not believe in cremation of the body at death. They consider that death is a form of pollution, and that the fire, therefore, would be contaminated by the corpse. Because the body in death is vulnerable to being penetrated by evil spirits, a corpse is anointed with nirangdeen to purify it. It cannot be thrown into the sea or river because it would make the sacred water unclean; it cannot be buried because it would make the sacred earth unclean also. So the body is isolated until it can be placed in the "dakhma." This is a huge stone tower that is open at the top so the body is exposed to vultures. After the bones are picked clean, they are taken to a pit where prayers are recited for the soul of the deceased.

In the meantime, while the body is being tended, the soul sits for three days near the head of the body. If the deceased has led a life of goodness, the soul is happy; otherwise, the soul is miserable. At dawn on the fourth day, a sweet wind from the South blows and the soul goes to the bridge that leads to Heaven. Beneath the bridge lies Hell. If the soul is that of a person who has led a good moral life, he is met by a beautiful maiden (his conscience) who leads him to Ahura-Mazda and a reception with honor. If the soul belongs to a person who has chosen evil in his life, he is met at the bridge by an ugly old hag who pushes him off the bridge into Hell, called the Abode of Falsehood.

Parsees do not allow anyone to become a member of their religion unless they have been born into it. They believe it is the best religion in the world and do not want it to be dissipated by people who may be ignorant and are dissatisfied with their own creed. They fear that the religion of Zoroaster would thereby become less than it is and would perhaps return to idol worship or worse.

Buddhism

During the time that Zoroaster was persuading the aristocracy of Persia to renounce wealth and search for truth, a Hindu prince of India named Siddhartha Gautama also rejected his life of luxury to search for the meaning of life.

Gautama was born 563 B.C. in a palace on the plains of the Ganges River at the foot of the great Himalaya Mountains. His father, who was king of the Sakyas Clan of Hindus, had reached the age of fifty without having a son to succeed him, and so he was very happy when the Prince was born. Seven holy wise men of the Himalayas who came to see the newborn prince predicted that "if he chooses a worldly life, he will be king of the world.''

Although his mother, Maya, died when he was very young, Gautamak's protective father saw to it that his education was as complete as possible. He learned to ride, to shoot with bow and arrows, to manage elephants and wild horses. At the age of twelve, he took the Sacred Thread of Hinduism and was educated by the best priests available in religious studies as well as in literature, grammar, math and astronomy. Religion was emphasized, and high caste boys learned from the Sanskrit texts of the Vedas, sacred books of the Hindus.

Although privileged and wealthy, the Prince was a gentle and compassionate boy. A story is told of how he usually played with his cousins, some of whom he liked better than others. Once when very small, he was playing with his least favorite cousin, Devadattha, whom he didn't like much because of his boastfulness. Devadattha pushed a bamboo wand upright into the ground and challenged the Prince to a contest of hitting it with arrows from their bows. Devadattha shot first and just missed hitting the wand. Then the Prince shot and split the wand down the middle with his arrow. His cousin became furious and angrily shot again, this time wildly and with a shot that struck a passing bird and caused it to fall to the ground. The Prince quickly picked up the injured bird and cradled it in his hands until it recovered from the shock, then he released it. Devadhattha argued that the bird was his to keep since he had ''caught'' it. The Prince replied that only when you heal and restore life can you say it belongs to you, not when you injure or take it away.

On the day the Prince was born, six other babies and a colt were also born in that kingdom, five males and one female. The five males later became his followers, the colt his favorite horse, and the female, the Princess Yosodhara, his bride at the age of sixteen. The couple were given three beautiful castles by the king and therein they lived happily for about ten years. Then the Prince became deeply affected by some observations he made.

One day while returning from hunting with his bodyguard, Channah, he saw a man, all skin and bones, writhing in pain on the ground. He asked Channah, "Why?" and was told that like many others, this man of lower caste was poor and sick. He said, ''That is how life is.''

The next day, while riding back to the palace again, they saw an old, old man bent as a bow, trembling and barely able to walk with two canes. When asked to explain, Channah said, ''That is how old age is.''

The third day they happened onto a funeral procession of weeping relatives. Channah once more explained, ''That is how death is. The life of every man, prince or pauper, ends in death.''

The Prince became very sad and, instead of attending the feast prepared for him by his Princess, retired to his private rooms to meditate and study the scriptures again to see whether he could understand why there had to be so much suffering in life, especially among the lower castes. It seemed to him that all pleasures were temporary and uncertain, while only suffering and death were permanent and sure.

The next day he went to the marketplace to be among people of all castes. This was a new experience for him, since he had always been sheltered from ugliness and poverty by his parents and teachers. There in the marketplace he observed a monk who was obviously elderly and very poor, but his face bore the expression of a calm and happy person. After reflecting on this experience and all he had seen, Gautama decided that he would live the life of a monk.

The Blessed Night of the Great Renunciation

So at the age of twenty-nine, with all the wealth and power of a kingdom his, he left his dear wife and new-born son in the palace and rode off with Channah into the wilderness. Once away from the kingdom, he shaved his head and beard, exchanged clothes with a beggar, and sent his weeping bodyguard back to the palace while he rode off alone. This event is remembered annually by all Buddhists and is called "The Blessed Night of the Great Renunciation."

For seven years he wandered about in search of wisdom, observing and talking to people of all castes. As he traveled, his reputation for gentle, simple, and wise philosophy and speech spread, and many people sought him out to talk with him. Among these folks was

Bimbisara, the good king of Mogadah. He so admired Gautama's ideas and demeanor that he invited him, a beggar, to become the king's advisor. The Prince refused, but promised to return and share with the king any knowledge he would gain by continuing to travel.

As he continued his journey, he visited many famous Hindu teachers, such as Udaka and Alara. Their advice was to study the Vedas for answers, but the Prince already had done this and he was dissatisfied, for the Holy Books encouraged castes in a world created by Brahman but without fairness to all men alike.

When he appealed to some monks he met for advice, they advised him to torture and starve his body, saying that such treatment would improve his vision and his soul. With the monks, he went into the forest and led a life of starvation and self-torture until he fainted one day and then could barely walk or talk. He concluded that self-torture was wrong, because it was when he fed and took care of his body that he could think most clearly.

The Prince's Enlightenment

By this time the Prince despaired of coming up with any answers about life's suffering and, in his discouraged mood, sat under a wild fig tree to think and decide what to do next. As he sat, he began to understand what he needed to know. He concluded that man is himself responsible for what is true in life. Good only comes from good actions done by man; evil comes from evil actions. This law, he felt, was the key.

Once he had this key, he remained meditating under the tree (later called the "Bo" or "wisdom" tree) for seven times seven days. Then he returned to the monks and shared his newfound knowledge with them. This first sharing was his "Sermon at Benares," and from this time, he became known as the Buddha, which means "The Enlightened One."

Though it was radically different, the new philosophy of Buddha was listened to and believed by the monks and other people. The Prince taught that the Vedas were not sacred God-given texts; they were wrong. Brahman did not create the world; it always had been and always would be. Gods could not change the world, so idol worship was wrong. Only man could change things by his acts of good and evil. And he emphasized that the caste system of inequality was evil. Especially important was his conclusion that extremes of hedonist and masochistic lifestyles were wrong. The middle path of moderation is what man needed to follow, a conclusion shared by the advocates of many other religions.

In the tradition established by Buddha following his Enlightenment, teaching and the subsequent sharing of knowledge ("dharma") have become the focus of the Buddhist religion. After his sermon to the monks, Buddha kept his promise to return to King Bimbisara. The King listened to Buddha's message, then he in turn taught others, and Buddhism spread throughout the kingdoms of

India. Word of him reached the Prince's home kingdom and he was asked to return. There the king and queen became converts to his way, along with Princess Yosodhara, his wife, who became the first Buddhist nun, and his son, Prince Rahula, who became a disciple.

The Buddha's reputation for being a wise and enlightened teacher continued to spread. A story is told to exemplify his gentle way of teaching:

There was a mother whose son had died. In her grief, she came to the Buddha and asked him, in his great wisdom, to restore her beloved son to life. Buddha said, "I can help you on one condition. Can you bring me a mustard seed from a house where neither child, parent, relative nor servant has died?"

Other legends attributed miraculous occurrences to Buddha's life. In one case, he is said to have tossed his rice bowl into a stream where it floated upstream against the current. In another case, the straw on which he and his disciples meditated mysteriously became a beautiful altar. With his reputation as a teacher well-established, the well-loved Buddha continued to teach and travel for forty-four years until he died in 483 B.C. at the age of eighty.

Buddha taught that enlightenment, the answer to life's suffering, lies in an individual's realizing four basic Noble Truths:

1) Suffering - Birth, illness, old age, frustration at not getting what one wants, and death are five areas of clinging to existence, that cause pain in life.

2) Cause of Pain - Pain comes from craving, lust for existence .

3) Cessation of Pain - Cessation involves doing away with craving.

4) Path to Cessation of Pain - This is an Eight-Fold Path,leading to the Middle Path of moderation and peace.

This Eight-Fold Path consists of:

1. Right Belief - Truth is man's guide.

2. Right Resolve - Be calm always and do no harm to an living creature.

3. Right Speech - Speak no lies, slander, coarse or harsh language.

4. Right Behavior - Do not kill, steal, commit adultery or drunkenness.

5. Right Occupation - Choose honorable work; no usury, forgery etc.

6. Right Effort - Always try for good; eschew evil.

7. Right Contemplation - Be calm; don't let joy or sorrow dominate you.

8. Right Concentration - Try to reach a superconscious state of perfect peace by following the seven steps, lose desire for material things, achieve inner contentment.

This goal of reaching a state wherein one is free from craving, suffering and sorrow transcends birth and death and is called Nirvana. Everyone is in a process of continual change. Everything is moving, transitory and part of a larger universal interdependent causality that is more important than the individual. Because of this, it is important to feel compassion and empathy for others who are also part of one gigantic whole. Therefore, part of our mutual responsibility is to help others by sharing our knowledge. Like Hindus, Buddhists believe in reincarnation, but they deny that the same self goes from one life to the next one. Where the soul goes after death is uncertain to Buddhists, but some believe that it is guided into another stage of consciousness. Others believe that is reincarnated on this planet elsewhere.

Buddhist Monks

When a child is about four, he may experience a preliminary ceremony of Buddhism. After his head is shaved, he is dressed in monk-like garb and is given a begging bowl to carry for part of the day. When he is about twenty, he may decide to become a monk; a girl may become a nun. In ancient times, this decision was a commitment for life. Now young people may enter the monastery for a few months only in order to learn about the faith. In Thailand and Cambodia, for example, all young men spend at least one rainy season in the Sangha (fellowship) of monks to learn the morals of Buddhism. In Burma (Myanmar), every village has at least one monastery.

Buddhist monks traditionally wear saffron robes and have shaved heads. The nuns wear white robes and also shave their hair. This removal of all hair from the head is at once a symbol of humility, the eschewing of vanity, and an act of discipline. Monks live austere lives of poverty, chastity and defenselessness according to the Code of Vinaya (rules).

The soliciting and giving of alms to monks is a recognized and honorable tradition. Their food is obtained by begging. In exchange, monks and nuns teach, do social service, and provide moral leadership for villagers. Buddhist monks are sometimes called "bonzis," "bhikkus," or "phongyis."

The texts of Buddhism are not extensive. There is *The Tripitake*, which consists of three parts:
1, 227 rules of discipline (Vinaya)
2. Discourses
3. Psychological and philosophical treatises.
These are all sermons and sayings of Buddha.

There is also the original preserved *Canon of the School of Elders* which is a Theravada text that was written in 25 B.C. in an Indic language called Pali.

The Divisions of Buddhism

About one hundred years after the death of Prince Gautama, disciples of Buddha began to disagree on how to carry on with his teaching. Today we see the results of

HOTEI-One of the seven Buddhist gods of luck. A cheerful deity, usually depicted with a naked stomach and a kindly expression, often pictured with children.

this disagreement and split; there are about forty different sects of Buddhism. The two largest divisions are the Mahayana Buddhism, which is found mainly in China, Korea and Japan. The Mahayana adherents strive to be active teachers like Buddha who can help others reach Nirvana. Theravada Buddhists, on the other hand, concentrate on their own salvation by strictly adhering to the ancient texts and the Eight-Fold Path.

Buddhism came to China in the first century A.D. when the Emperor Ming had a dream. He dreamed about a man of golden aura who descended to Earth from the sun via a shaft of sunlight, and who conquered the Earth with his beauty of spirit and his ideas. The astrologers of the court interpreted the man of gold to be Buddha, and so the Emperor was converted to Buddhism, along with all of his Empire.

Buddhism in Tibet is unique in that it developed in conjunction with an ancient animism called Bon which paid homage to many gods of nature and the underworld by magic and sacrifices of animals and humans. In the eighth century A.D., Tibetans changed and began to follow the teachings of Prince Gautama's disciples as administered by their priests who were called lamas. Because they believed their lamas were divinely reincarnated to succeed themselves, the chief priest, called the Dalai Lama, was worshipped by Tibetans. In 1960, when the Chinese Communists overran their country, the Dalai Lama left Tibet with one hundred followers. After this exodus, a rival Panchen Lama took his place.

Of the forty different sects of Buddhism, there are many that, in spite of his teaching to the contrary, have set up images of the Buddha for worship. Today we see many figures of Buddha, sitting, standing or reclining, Great temples have been built in his honor. In Rangoon, Myanmar, for instance, the Shwe Dagon temple has a multi-spired roof of gold. The spires are covered with fine gold leaf, bits of which have been contributed by pilgrims to honor their idol. In some temples, relics of Buddha are revered, such as his footprints and his sandals. The Temple of the Sacred Tooth stands in Kandy, Sri Lanka.

*The world's largest outdoor bronze Buddha which sits
seven stories tall on Lantau Island, Hong Kong.*

Zen Buddhism

One very popular sect of Buddhism is called Zen. Begun in China about one thousand years after Buddha lived, it was first known as Ch'an, which means "meditation." It was changed to Zan, then Zen, and continues to emphasize the importance of concentration, often achieved through yoga. The goal of Zen is to realize the Buddhist nature in oneself that is ideally in harmony with the universe. However, Zen advocates stress that there should be no set pattern to the religious experience; they teach that thoughts and actions are more important than structure. A popular Zen saying is, "If you meet the Buddha on the road, kill him!" In other words, don't worship Buddha; strive rather for an awareness of what is true and right for you.

There are many stories to illustrate Zen philosophy. One tells of a pilgrim who comes to a Zen monk saying that he wants to find the Buddha. The monk takes a pail of water and dumps it over the pilgrim's head. When asked why, he says that his action is just as sensible as the pilgrim's request to be told how to "find" Buddha.

Another tale is about two men, one young and one old, who are standing by a stream about to cross. A beautiful girl comes and asks for help in getting across the water. The old man carries her across the stream. Later that day, the young man says that he thinks it was wrong of the old man to carry the young girl. "Oh," says the old man, "I carried her only a few minutes across the water. You, on the other hand, have been carrying her in your mind all day.''

In the Buddhist year, there are frequent holidays and festivals. New Years is especially important, as is a holiday called Wesak, which is usually celebrated in May. This festival commemorates the birth, enlightenment and death of Buddha.

Buddhist philosophy stresses social service, and so there are many orphanages, hospitals and schools that have been started by Buddhists. A Buddhist who foregoes his own search for Nirvana in order to help others find theirs is called a Bodhisattra.

Unlike Hinduism, wherein you have to be born to belong, Buddhism welcomes converts of all races, nationalities and colors. Today there are about 311,438,000 Buddhists, mostly living in Myanmar (Burma), Thailand, Sri Lanka and Tibet, as well as in China, Japan and in North and South America. There are very few Buddhists today in India, the land where it all began.

No spot of Earth but is a shrine,
Be it the vast expanse of ocean waste,
Or highest mountain's summit sun-caressed,
In all resides the power divine.

The Shinto Way of Life

We know that animism was the worship of the spirits of natural objects and phenomena by primitive people. The spiritual way of life for most Japanese people today is directly rooted in animism. The word, "Shinto," is derived from two Chinese words and means literally, "the way of the gods." Although its history goes back a thousand years before, it was named in the fifth or sixth century in order to distinguish it from Buddhism and Confucianism which came on the scene at that time in the island communities of Japan.

Shinto is not considered a religion by some people because there is no clearly defined strict code of behavior involved. There is no ultimate heaven or paradise, no sin and no punishment. It is, rather, an attempt to recognize that man is part of the natural world and as such, must live in harmony with the kindness and benevolence of Mother Nature.

There was no prophet, creator or ruler involved in the rise of Shintoism. It evolved in ancient Japan by primitive hunters, fishermen, and farmers who relied on nature for survival, and who learned to live in peace with an environment which was friendly to them. They considered themselves blessed with beautiful mountains, water and forests. They were right, because compared to the mid-Eastern deserts, birthplace of most other spiritual movements, theirs was a very pleasant and easy environment.

The Kami

The Shinto myth of creation begins before the Earth took shape. All matter, they say, was then an amorphous mass floating about in space. Out of this mass developed the first of the Kamis (spirits, deities). These Kamis selected two of their number, Izanagi and Izanami, to give form to the Earth.

Izanagi and Izanami stood one day on the Floating Bridge of Heaven (the rainbow) and stirred the oceans with a jeweled sword. Then they held up the sword and let it drip. The drops formed the eight islands of Japan.

The Eight Island Nation was Japan's first name.

Izanagi and Izanami then descended to Earth, built a palace and erected a Pillar of Heaven. When they discovered their sexual differences, that they were male and female, they mated and gave birth to children, the first ones of whom were deficient because the female Kami had been the one who decided to mate. When they repeated the mating at the suggestion of the male, they had normal Kami children from whom eventually evolved Amaratsu, the Sun Goddess.

Ninigi-No-Mikoto, grandson of Amaterasu, became the patriarch of the imperial line of human Japanese emperors. The first of these emperors was Jimmu Tenno, who was born in 711 B.C. and took the throne in 660 B.C.. Belief that the emperor is directly descended from the Sun Goddess still exists among some people of Japan; Japanese people generally have great respect for the emperor.

The Kami of Shinto are more spirits than gods. They are beings that are superior to man , somewhat like Christian and Islamic angels, but are different in that they also exist in his heart and mind as forces which make man creative and progressive. They are consistently friendly. There are no evil Kami, and they are similar to men in that they are sexual. This is illustrated in the Shinto myth that man was born of Kami originally. Unlike many gods, the Kami require no sacrifice, though they are offered gifts of food and sake in the Shinto shrines.

Altogether there are over eight hundred Kami! There

are Kami that are abstract, such as the Kami of growth, fertility and productivity. There are Kami of natural phenomena, like wind, thunder and rain. Some Kami are associated with natural objects such as the Kami of the sun, mountains, trees, rivers and rocks. There are Kami of animals, such as dogs, foxes, wolves, tigers, hares and crows. Some families have ancestral Kami, especially imperial families. Clans of people usually have their particular Kami, and there are regional Kamis of commu-

Mitsumine Wolf Shrine (Shinto) in Saitama, Japan.

nities or even of particular needs, such as childbirth and the passing of exams.

Unlike the gods of some religions who work in opposition to each other, all the Kami work together in unity to create the harmony of the cosmos, the way of nature.

There are over 100,000 shrines in Japan where people go to pay respect to Kami. The new Japanese word for shrine is "jinja" but the older word, "miya" is still also popularly used. Long ago religious ceremonies were held outside, but today this is unusual and rarely seen.

When there is an outdoor ritual, it takes place in an area of evergreen trees that is set off by a sacred straw rope and circled by stones. In the center is a sacred tree which is called a "himorogi," and into this area the Kami is invited to come. Ceremonies used to be held at night, but the consumption of wine and sake during the ceremonies too often led to immoral behavior, so now they are always held during daylight hours.

Festivals with rituals are held for many reasons: increasing of the food supply, quieting of souls, or appeasing or stroking some particular Kami such as the Kami of fire or water. The ceremony always involves prayers led by a priest; these prayers are prayers of praise, petition or gratitude. Along with prayers, there are offerings of wine, sake and food. No blood is ever visible on the meat offerings because visible blood is considered pollution. There is music and dancing, after which there is usually a feast and sharing of food, wine and sake. Demonstrations of magic are sometimes included in the ceremony.

Purification Rituals

Purification is very important to Shinto and is the basis for the Japanese love of communal bathing. Some purification or cleansing process is present in many religions and is sometimes done with water splashing or immersion, but the washing is symbolic for the cleansing of the spirit. Salt is sometimes sprinkled on people who have attended a funeral because death signifies decay and pollution. The salt or saltwater bathing is supposed to cleanse people and prepare them to resume a normal life. At the entrance to most shrines is found a fountain for rinsing the hands or mouth before entering. Water is considered to be the flowing force of life, and so is used to bring about change, renewal and freshness in a symbolic way.

The need for frequent purification or cleansing stems from the basic belief that while people are not good or bad, they can sometimes fall into a state of impurity. Purification cleanses away any polluting spirits or presences that cause this state. Along with the use of water for cleansing, a priest may chant prayers for the recipient while he waves the "ohari," a stick to which have been attached white cut papers, symbolic of the cleansing force.

The TORII - a typical entrance to a Shinto shrine, separating the mundane world of man from the spiritual world of Kami.

Besides performing the rites of purification, Shinto priests preside at festivals, lead people in prayers, and teach and interpret the ethics of Shinto. Their positions were originally hereditary, and succession now is reverting back to that method which for some years had not been followed.

Basic to the ethics of Shinto is the belief that human nature is good, and that the Kami are also good. There is no evil inherent in men or Kami, but there are sometimes distortions, results of bad interpersonal and environmental conditions. But although man is imperfect, he is capable of growth and with help can achieve serenity and peace of mind. Though there is no heaven or paradise to reach toward, man can create on Earth a dynamic and flourishing harmony with nature and be successful in life.

Japanese myths used for teaching Shintoists stress the need to respect nature and not to abuse its gifts. According to a popular legend, a very rich man had so many rice fields that he could not have them all planted by sundown in one day, so he commanded the sun not to set until all was done. The sun obeyed, but the next day when the man looked out over his fields, he saw only a huge lake where his rice fields had been.

Shinto teaches what is called the situational ethic. This means that there is no one way of doing the right thing, unvaried, at all times. Man must try to have purity of motivation in his heart and mind resulting from meditation and purification. It is also important for both men and Kami to cultivate ''makoto,'' which means honesty, conscientiousness, and truthfulness in all their habits and dealings with other men. Man is never required to do more than what he is capable of doing, but he must do his best under the particular circumstances.

Today there are more than 3,205,300 members of Shinto, mostly living in Japan. Its expenses there are paid by the imperial family, not by the government. In the United States, there are about 48,000 members. Modern day Shinto is often blended with the tenets of Buddhism and Confucianism, and it is not unusual for a Japanese to practise all three.

This poem written by a Shinto priest epitomizes this modern but ancient form of worship:

No spot of Earth but is a shrine,
Be it the vast expanse of ocean waste,
Or highest mountain's summit sun-caressed,
In all resides the power divine.

Let there be no evil
in your thoughts.

Confucius

Like the early Japanese primitive people, the Chinese of long ago were worshippers of the gods of natural forces that controlled the way they lived. Being farmers, they revered the sun, the rain, and the spirit of fertility that made their crops and animals flourish. Because the sun, rain, clouds and rainbow were in the sky, they concluded that there must be one supreme god who was in charge of all gods and men and who lived in heaven, somewhere in the firmament. This god they called T'ien. Because there was so much to oversee, he had a lesser god, Shang-ti, whose job was to watch over people.

Along with these gods of nature, the ancient Chinese paid homage to the spirits of their ancestors and dead heroes, who they felt could help them in time of need. For example, when people living during the time of the Shang Dynasty (1700-1051 B.C.) had a major problem, they often appealed to their ancestors for help by writing questions on animal bones. Then they would throw the bones into a fire to roast until the bones cracked. After being cooled, the cracks would be studied and read for answers.

The other focus of their worship was the emperor. He was believed to be divinely inspired and holy, therefore having greater access to the gods. We know that two thousand years before Christ, these emperors were often counseled by wise men called sages, who also served as teachers of the people.

Two of these sages, Yu and Tang, were especially respected for their good advice to people on how to live in the world. The essence of what they taught was that if people follow right and try to be good, they would be fortunate in all their endeavors.

The Birth of Confucius

Yu and Tang were often quoted and so immortalized by K'ung-Fu-Tze (Confucius), who lived a long time after them and who became China's most famous teacher. In 551 B.C., legend relates that Ching-Tsai, the fifteen-year-old pregnant concubine of Shu-Liang-Ho, a seventy-five-year-old soldier and provincial governor, dreamed that her child would be born in the Hollow Mulberry Tree Cave. This cave was near the village of Chow in the state of Lu, the province of Shantung.

Ching-Tsai went alone to the cave, and on September 27, 551 B.C., her son, Confucius, was born. On the night of his birth, two friendly dragons circled the skies to protect mother and child from evil. With the dragons were five sages disguised as planets who were directed by a voice from heaven to surround the holy place of birth. After delivering the baby boy, Ching-Tsai wrapped him up and walked with him into the village. As she walked, the trees bowed down to worship.

This legend and others like it evolved after Confucius' life and death. It reveals how the Chinese came to worship the man in a religion named after him, although he never intended that this should be. He simply sought to teach people and especially politicians how to live morally and well.

His father died when Confucius was three years old. His mother raised him alone, making his education a top priority. At the age of nineteen, Confucius married, not very happily, and had a son and daughter of his own. As a young man, he worked as a tithing master accountant who recorded tenants' grain donations to their feudal lord. Then he became the keeper of a granary and later, an administrator of public works.

Chief Magistrate of Lu

When he was twenty-three years old, his mother died and he left his job to mourn for three years (27 months) as was the custom. After the mourning period, he decided to teach. His reputation as a wise and thoughtful teacher spread, and he was asked by the Prince of Lu to be the Chief Magistrate (Justice) of a village. In this capacity, he emphasized putting good people in positions of authority in order to set examples for those who were governed. The system worked; the crime rate dropped to zero and the jails of the village all became and remained empty. Confucius said, "Government consists of the correct choice of officials. One must elevate the just men so they can exert pressure upon crooked men, for in this way the crooked may be made straight." The Prince of Lu was pleased and life in his state was very good.

After a while, neighboring princes observed the changes in the state of Lu. They became afraid that they would lose power over their own people, so they plotted together to ruin the Prince of Lu. They sent him gifts of beautiful harem girls and racehorses.

The plot worked. Soon the prince was spending all his time with the girls and the horses, letting the affairs of state be neglected. Eventually the government was in shambles and he lost control entirely. Confucius left the state to travel and teach elsewhere.

Confucius as Teacher

Although he could not ever attain a position of high authority from which he could influence the warring feudal lords to share his sense of social responsibility, Confucius became known and loved by the common people. This peripatetic teacher often rode in a bullock cart while his students walked alongside and listened as he described his dream of "a society of gentle superior people living in the truth of righteousness."

These people, he taught, would pursue five basic things:

1. True recognition of duties
2. Knowledge
3. Respect of ancestors
4. Awareness of their potential
5. Love.

Gentlemanliness was very important to Confucius. He defined a gentleman as one who is at least troubled by his own shortcomings, even when he has difficulty overcoming them. He said, "The demands a gentleman makes are on himself. Those a small man makes are upon others." He also taught, "The superior man understands what is right; the inferior man understands what will sell."

In order to have success in the ways of "Jen," which was explained as "all that is good in man" or "love," he suggested that a man should be observant, courteous, respectful of his parents, and lead a quiet life that is reverent of all living things.

To illustrate his conception of courtesy, he would not allow paper to be discarded if there were calligraphy or printing that someone had done on it.

On the subject of parental respect he said, "Though a man may never before have revealed himself, he is certain to do so when mourning for a mother or a father."

In regard to all relationships he commented that a man must be "in private life, courteous, in public life, diligent, in all relationships, loyal."

He emphasized the importance of the Golden Rule i.e. doing unto others as you would have them do unto you.

Along with the Golden Rule and the Code of Jen, Confucius taught the Code of Li, which applies to a man's role in the culture and his social virtues as practised in observing the rules of ritual and protocol. "Li" means "giving room to others."

An important facet of Li was realizing that one had to study in order to know how to be a good member of society. Confucius had a lot to say about education. For instance, "True manhood consists in realizing your true self and in restoring universal values. Whosoever will realize his true self and restore universal values, the world will follow him." This realization of self comes with study and application of what one has studied and learned. "Learning undigested by thought is labor lost; thought unassisted by learning is dangerous." The danger of learning for the wrong reasons was addressed when he said, "In the old days men studied for the sake of self-improvement; nowadays men study in order to impress other people."

The most important theme of the master's teaching was his repeated warning that people must consistently and always try to make decisions that were morally good. A popular Confucian proverb states: "In your secret chamber even you are judged; see you do nothing to blush for, though but the ceiling looks down upon you." When asked to select one phrase that would best sum up the philosophy of his instruction, he said, "Let there be no evil in your thoughts."

Texts of Confucius

There are many books written by and about Confucius. His best known work is probably *The Analects (Lun Yu)* which consists of a series of conversations with Confucius. He also wrote five classics called *K'ing* or *Ching* which are distillations of the religious lore of the ancients plus his own observations on spiritualism. The final one of the five is *The Book of Spring and Autumn (Ch'un Ch'iu)* which was written after he knew that he was dying. It is his recording of events in the state of Lu before and during his life. Many scholars have written interpretations of Confucianism. About one hundred years after Confucius lived, a disciple named Mencius

Confucius

wrote *The Book Mencius (Menq-tze)*. He was a well-respected teacher and became known as the Second Sage of China, Confucius having been the First Sage.

Confucius died in 479 B.C. at the age of eighty. Although he never intended to be known as a saint or messiah, it was not long before his disciples effected his apotheosis (deification). Many of them spent three years mourning at his grave on the bank of the river Szu in the state of Chow. There they offered sacrifices of sheep and cattle. Some built huts and remained there for the rest of their lives. His days of birth and death became days of ceremony and sacrifice.

Two hundred fifty years after his death, Emperor Ts'in Shih Hwang-ti came to power and declared himself to be the first real emperor of China. He decreed that his subjects must erase all previous rulers from their memories. In his quest for greater absolute power he mobilized the army and used it to conquer lands in the north and the south. Then he ordered the burning of all books and the execution of five hundred scholars who would remember the books and the events of the past.

Their books were very heavy and cumbersome compared to ours today. They were made from slips of bamboo one inch by two feet on which writing was done in a kind of varnish. Holes in the corners provided for fastening together the "pages" with silk or leather thongs. The fire from the emperor's book burning, including many works of Confucius, consequently lasted for three months!

·When the Emperor Ts'in Shih Hwang-ti died, the people of China (from Ts'ina, which he had named his empire), brought out the books they had hidden in the walls of their houses and named the dead emperor, "The Criminal of Ten Thousand Generations!"

Today there are about 5,821,400 followers of Confucianism in Red China, Taiwan, Southeast Asia and North and South America.

Confucius might be appalled to see his simple and wise teachings formalized into the complex rituals and superstitions coupled with the critical rationalism that seeks to worship the man instead of living by his message.

Since the takeover of China by the Communists, there is little tolerance for foreign religions or missionaries. But the worship of Confucius is allowed at home altars or ancestral shrines. Although Communism professes that any religion is the result of immaturity and superstition, Chinese Communists respect Confucius as a part of their history. Therefore they allow his books to be read. Some Chinese today say that the spirit of the Master - Confucius - is pervasive in the Chinese culture, just under the surface. They say that Chinese people try to live as Confucius taught, that is, by trying to "will the right, hold (onto) the good won, rest in love and move in art."

Taoism

The three philosophies of Confucius, Buddha and Lao-Tze are so compatible that a person can live according to all three without conflict. Because so many Chinese people embrace all of the three teachings, Confucianism, Taoism, and Buddhism (called Omito Fo in China), it is difficult to number Taoists, but there are at least fifty million of them today. Most of them live in China, Korea and Manchuria, with ten to fifteen thousand in the United States.

Unlike Buddhists, a Taoist does not expect to find salvation by an ultimate state of peace that is union with what is infinite i.e. Nirvana. What he is encouraged to find in this religion is the way to spend his life in the world in a personally satisfactory way.

In contrast to Confucianism, which emphasizes that the way to learn how to do this is by education, Taoism teaches that man already has this innate knowledge; all he must do is to bring it to the surface of his consciousness and apply it in his every-day life.

We know little about the beginning of Taoism, but we do know that it began in the sixth century B.C. in China with the birth and philosophy of Lao-Tze. One legend calls him Li Erh. His name was Li-Peh-Yand when he was born into the poor family of Li in Keuh village, Le Parish, Tsow District, some time in the sixth century B.C..

Nothing is known about his life until he was a young man who was employed as Keeper of the Royal Archives in the city of Lo-Yang. There he worked for most of his adult life at his job of tending the royal library. As he worked, he read a great deal and expressed opinions about what he learned. His reputation for wisdom grew, and people eventually named him Lao-Tze, which means "The Old Philosopher."

He probably would have remained in the royal library until he died, except it happened that his provincial ruler became corrupt and began to act in dishonorable ways. Lao-Tze refused to work for him anymore and left the province. As he approached the provincial border, he was questioned by the border guards. When they learned that he was "The Old Philosopher," they insisted that he could not leave until he had put into writing some of what he had been teaching. So Lao-Tze sat down and wrote the five-thousand-page *Tao-Teh-King (Book of Virtue)*, the shortest religious book in the world. Then he disappeared forever.

The Book of Virtue is obscurely written and difficult to interpret, but many Taoists have written lengthy volumes of their explanations of Lao-Tze's philosophy. Unfortunately each one came to his own conclusions, and so the religion of Taoism has taken many different paths, most of them vastly different from what he had taught. Like the followers of Prince Gautama Buddha and Prince Mahavira, the Jain, the descendants of Lao-Tse created idols and other ways to worship the teacher instead of emphasizing his message.

Lao-Tze's Philosophy

Lao-Tze's philosophy was not complicated. "To be good," he taught, "follow Tao and the world will take care of itself." There are many definitions for Tao: the Way, the Path, the Word, reason, and God. Another way of describing Tao is to call it the combination of the negative force of Yin and the positive force of Yang. These two are the basic principles of the universe which operate through water, fire, soil, wood, and metal to produce all the phenomena of the Earth and man's actions thereon. Lao-Tze stressed that all men are born good and need only apply what they know innately in order to remain good. He wrote, "A truly good man loves all men and hates none." He stressed a lesson which is also emphasized in Christianity when he advised, "Repay injury with kindness; repay evil with good." In his own life he stated, "To those who are good to me, I am good. To those who are not good to me, I am good. Thus all get to be good."

He was much opposed to imprisonment and capital punishment for criminals. He said the only way to reform people was to be kind to them. War, to Lao-Tze, was senseless and he said, "The great objective of the good man is to keep peace. He takes no pleasure in winning battles and in killing his fellow men."

Magic in Taoism

After Lao-Tze's death, the various interpretations of his text evolved into many different sects of Taoism. Some of the new leaders tried to adhere to his emphasis on goodness and kindness as the key. Others chose to interpret his often obscure writings as a license for encouraging superstitious practises and the use of magic.

For example, one Taoist of the second century, A.D., Chang-Tao-Ling (Celestial Teacher), claimed to have discovered a potion that would make people live forever. People believed in him and consequently began to worship him. Among his followers was the infamous Emperor Ts'in (The Criminal of Ten Thousand Generations). This man, who had ordered the burning of all Confucius' books, allowed the books of Taoism to remain because he wanted to know the secret of how to live forever. When the potion of immortality failed, Chang offered all kinds of excuses.

Another of the legends about the search for immortality in Taoism says that there were people who never died living in the mountains of Central Asia where they were ruled by Hsi-Wang-Mu, the Queen of the West. In her garden was a peach tree that bore fruit once every thousand years. Those who ate of this fruit would never die. Still another legend recounts that all immortals eventually go to live on the moon.

Chang-Tao-Ling and later, his decendants, came to be known as the Pearly Emperors.. He lived in the Dragon-Tiger Mountains near Kang-Si where he ruled his followers like a king. His subjects believed in demons, vampires, goblins and other evil spirits and sought protection from them. They sometimes worshipped idols as well as dragons, rats, weasels and snakes. Certain stones were supposed to protect them from drowning, ashes protected them from fire, and various words written on paper protected them from bullets.

When entering the forest, believed to be the haunt of wood devils, people would sing or whistle to ward them off. To protect themselves in the house, they would build the foyer crooked and then paint a forest mural where the entrance was so that any evil spirit who tried to run into their house would dash into the wall! The worst evil demons inhabited the mountains; the bigger the mountain was, the more wicked the demon was supposed to be.

Evil spirits often roamed the Earth in disguise. A legend is told about Pih-He, a good magician who went to stay at an inn at the foot of Li Lu Mountain. It was known that anyone who stayed overnight at this inn would never live to tell about it.   Pih-He sat reading one evening by candlelight in the central room of the inn when the door opened and in came ten tall men dressed in black. They sat down and started to gamble. Pih-He looked into his magic mirror and was startled to see ten dogs where the men were sitting! He walked around the room with his candle and suddenly thrust the candle toward one of the gamblers. He smelled singed dog hair, so he drew his knife and slew one of the men. The other nine ran away, and there on the floor lay a dead dog!

Belief in magic was an important part of the religion practise of the followers of Chang Chueh, who was another early Taoist leader. They believed in spirits, both good ones (the Shen) and bad ones (the Kwei). The bad spirits could sometimes be controlled by magic charms and with the help of fortune-tellers and geomancers. The good spirits could fall down on the job and so they would have to be reminded about people's needs.

For example, if there were not enough rain for crops, the Taoists would make a huge paper dragon to represent the rain spirit. Then they would hold a huge noisy parade to wake up the dragon. If he did not respond to noise or bribery, they would sometimes tear him to pieces to punish him!

These followers of Chang Chueh, who were known by their yellow turbans, were reputed to be able to pass through stone and metal, as well as to walk through fire or on water. This particular sect that emphasized magic was so powerful and such a threat to the government that it was dispossessed by the Nationalist Army in 1927.

With the growing influence of Buddhism in the eighth century A.D., there developed a code of Taoism that addressed the matter of sin and compensatory good deeds. According to this code, some of which had been developed by Chang Chueh, a very sick person could cleanse himself of his sins by confessing them in a quiet place, then making offerings of wine, prayers and five measures of rice. The confession had to be copied three times. One copy was carried to the mountains, one copy was soaked in the river, and one copy was buried. In this way, the penitent was assured of communication with the Genii of Heaven, Earth and Water, so he would be cleansed of the sins by all three of them.

Every Taoist was supposed to have three genii in charge of him; these personal genii reported every fifty-seventh day of a sixty-day cycle to the gods. Yu-Huan-Shangti (The Jade Emperor) was the most important god. Under him served many lesser gods, goddesses and spirits. One very important god was Tai-Shun, who was in charge of local village and city gods. Every village had a temple to him and every city had a temple outside its eastern gate. This god also was the god of agriculture and ancestor worship.

Modern Taoists are roughly divided into those of the North and those of the South of China. Both embrace elements of Buddhism and Confucianism. In the North, the emphasis is on meditation, breathing and metaphysical speculation. In the South, there prevails an acceptance that man is just one part of all cosmic energy and his fate can be either peaceful or unfortunate. This philosophy can be described as a laissez-faire attitude of letting Nature take its course.

Generally, today's Taoists believe in a passive gentle acceptance of the Tao or Way of the universe. They are loyal and loving to each other, as well as careful not to injure grass, trees, insects, animals or any living thing. They, like Buddhists, believe that a person has to be rid of desire in order to be happy. The Taoist Creed says:

"He who knows other men is discerning;
He who knows himself is intelligent.
He who overcomes others is strong;
He who overcomes himself is mighty.
He who is satisfied with his lot is rich."

The Greeks and the Romans

At the time the Far and Middle Eastern civilizations were developing, the first settlers arrived by sea from Asia in what is now Greece. They first occupied the islands of Cyprus, Crete, some of the Cyclades, and the southeastern part of the Greek peninsula. These settlers were using Neolithic tools of stone and obsidian until 2900-2600 B.C. when the widespread use of copper and its natural alloys in the near east resulted in the advent of The Bronze Age (sometimes called The Copper Age).

The heritage of these settlers was a combination of agricultural, pastoral, and marine life. Religion in this new land centered around the worship of stumpy statuettes that represented female deities. In southern Greece, there is evidence dated 2000 B.C. that goddesses were worshipped, often attended by priestesses and animal-headed humans. The goddess cults sometimes associated themselves with sacred trees and animals, particularly snakes, bulls and doves.

At the same time, in the northern part of the peninsula, nomadic hunters from the Balkans were moving southward down the peninsula. With them they brought a new animal, the horse, and their own form of worship. In contrast to the south, their religion emphasized the male aspect, as evidenced in their male statuettes and many phallic symbols.

Eventually one hundred fifty-eight Greek city-states developed where the inhabitants honored their particular gods of state with statues, temples and festivals.

Because of intermittent volcanic destruction, our knowledge through artifacts of the oldest period in Greek history is limited. One of our most important sources is the 28,000 lines of Homer's epic poems, "The Iliad" and "The Odyssey," for which we do not an exact date. Historians generally agree, however, that 1200 B.C. was the date of that particular destruction of Troy which is recorded in these epics.

Another source of knowledge is the myths of Greece which tell us that long ago the Titans, children of Uranus (Heaven) and Gaia (Earth) were in charge of the world. The youngest Titan, Cronus, and his wife, Rhea, had a

The temple of Poseidon, God of the Sea, brother of Zeus, God of the Sea. Greek (c. 460 B.C.)

son named Zeus. To prevent Cronus from swallowing Zeus, Rhea sneaked him away to Crete where he grew up to become king of the gods on Mt. Olympus, with his queen, Hera.

There were twelve major Greek gods, dozens of lesser ones, and they were human-like, except that they never aged or died. These gods mingled with humans and sometimes married them. People worshipped them at home and in temples, and sometimes asked oracles (priest-ess mediators) to appeal to the gods for help. Some of the Greek rulers claimed to be divine themselves, and were so treated by the people.

The Beginning of Democracy

About the fifth century B.C., some of the Greek philosophers, writers, and teachers began to question the divine rights of the city-states' rulers and to emphasize the rights of individuals. Some important questioners were Euripedes, Aeschylus, Sophocles and Socrates; later there were Plato and Aristotle. Euripedes wrote ninety-two plays, many of which rejected the traditional acceptance of the power and infallibility of the gods. Aeschylus and Sophocles were also poets and playwrights who questioned the authorities of the times.

Socrates was a wise teacher who constantly attacked the most basic assumptions of his pupils in order to make them think He emphasized that all he personally could be sure of was that he "knew nothing." He was accused of making agnostics of young people. The government officials put him on trial for corrupting youthful morals when he encouraged them to question the worship of the gods of the state. Socrates refused to appeal his conviction and died by drinking poison hemlock.

Plato, Socrates' pupil, taught that man's immortal soul comes from a spiritual world of ideas before being born into an earthly body. Man should spend his time, he taught, seeking truth, beauty, and goodness. He needs to find perfect wisdom by remembering what is already known to him at birth, and by trying to live a life of courage and moderation. This temperate life style of the Greeks came to be known as "The Golden Mean."

Much later in the third century A.D., a Neo-Platonist named Plotinus stressed that there was indeed one ultimate spiritual essence or being with whom man should try to be reunited. He deviated from Platonism in that he incorporated in his teaching some of the basic tenets of Hinduism.

When the powerful Roman Empire expanded by conquering the Etruscans in Italy and then the Greeks in the first and second centuries B.C., the Romans came to admire many facets of the Greek culture. They therefore adopted much of it, particularly the alphabet and the Greek gods. The Romans renamed the Greek deities; Zeus and Hera became Jupiter and Juno, Aphrodite became Venus, and so on, but they were essentially the same gods and goddesses.

As the Roman emperors ascended to power, many of them presented themselves as being divine. Eventually, as had happened in Greece, there were Romans who questioned man's relationship to the gods. Some of these men were called Stoics, Epicureans and Skeptics. In 45 B.C., Marcus Tillius Cicero wrote *The Nature of Gods* as a discussion of these various viewpoints. His work was important because it questioned religion for meaning and not just for the elaborate rituals that were very popular at that time.

When Jerusalem, Palestine, was destroyed by the Romans in A.D. 70 to put down a Jewish rebellion there, Rome became the new center of Christianity. When the followers of Jesus Christ began to teach their lessons of Christianity in Rome, many of them were severely persecuted during the reigns of various emperors. They suffered especially at the time of Diocletian who was Emperor from A.D. 284 to 305. However, in A.D. 381, Emperor Theodosius I became converted to Christianity and forbade all other religions in the Roman Empire.

Many of the countries that were part of the Roman Empire have remained Christian countries to the present time. Ninety-seven and a half per cent of the Greeks today belong to the Eastern Orthodox Catholic Church and most Italians are Roman Catholics.

Christianity: Catholics and Protestants

Christians worship one God and recognize Jesus Christ to be the Son of God, who was born to Mary, a Jewish virgin and Joseph, her carpenter spouse, and who lived on Earth for thirty-three years as a human being. During that time, Jesus performed miracles, cured people who were sick and dying, taught his followers how to live morally, was executed by crucifixion, was resurrected, and finally returned to God.

After the Jews were settled in Palestine, they lived under a variety of conquering rulers, but they consistently believed in their tradition that promised the coming of a

Messiah who would teach them how to be saved and reach Heaven.

The Life of Jesus Christ

About the year A.D. 4, Jesus was born in a stable in Bethlehem, Judea, Palestine, to Mary and Joseph, who had traveled there in regard to payment of taxes to the Roman ruler. Angels appeared that night to some shepherds, and the angels declared Jesus to be the long-awaited Messiah and the Son of God. Not everyone believed this to be true.

We know that Jesus was raised in Galilee by Mary and Joseph, but not much is recorded about his childhood. When he became an adult, his cousin, John the Baptist, started preaching that the Jews should stop doing evil and return to the ways that God had revealed to them through Moses and the other prophets. John attracted much attention as he taught and baptized people, including Jesus, in the river Jordan. Then Jesus also began to preach in public, teaching about God and performing miracles of healing the sick, feeding the hungry, and in many ways demonstrating supernatural control over the forces of nature.

Many people came to believe in his message. His followers were called disciples, twelve of whom became his apostles and constant companions. The Jewish community leaders under the Roman ruler considered Jesus a troublemaker because he treated all classes of people as equal and made no secret of his contempt for wealth and earthly power.

This lesson was illustrated when the usually gentle man who preached the importance of love, threw the moneychangers out of the temple where they were doing business. He argued that the love of God and each other was more important than power, thus incurring the wrath of Jewish and Roman leaders.

After betrayal by Judas Iscariot, one of his apostles, Jesus was put to death by being hung on the cross like the common criminals of the time. Before he died, he forgave the people who killed him.

After burial in a tomb, he rose three days later and again walked among the people for forty days, repeating what he had taught about God and urging the Palestinians to follow his teachings.

The story of Jesus' life is told in four parallel versions by four of his adherents, Matthew, Mark, Luke and John. This story and related ones make up the New Testament of the Bible. Although Christians also believe in the validity of the Old Testament legends and prophecies, their creed emphasizes the lessons taught by Jesus, his divinity, his resurrection, and his promise of union with God for those who believe in Him.

Christian Beliefs

Christianity is a religion that stresses the love of a merciful God for all people and the need for humans to love and tolerate each other. Christians believe that the body dies, but the soul is immortal.

Since the beginning of Christianity, which encompasses a variety of classes and races of people, many of them poor, Christians have been periodically a socially persecuted group. In spite of this, and because Christ urged his disciples to travel and teach others, there are today 1,711,877,000 Christians. This constitutes the largest religious group in the world.

All Christians believe in one Creator who is sovereign of the universe. They believe that man was created in God's image, has rebelled, and will be judged by God, who is loving and merciful. The way to live morally has been revealed by God to people through the prophets of the Old and New Testaments, and by Christ's life and death. Jesus became the Incarnate (with a human body) Son of God, who died for men's salvation and was resurrected to prove that what he was teaching was true.

Christians believe in what is called the Holy Spirit or Holy Ghost, the third part of the Trinity. The Trinity means "one God in three forms." The idea of the Trinity originated in the early church to illustrate the all-encompassing power of God. There is God, the Omnipotent Father in Heaven; there is Jesus Christ, the Incarnate Son who lived as a man on Earth; and there is the Holy Spirit, which is the power of God working in the world around us.

Catholics

The largest Christian church is the Roman Catholic Church, with about 971,702,000 members. "Catholic" means "worldwide." Among the twelve original disciples, it was to Peter that Jesus said, "...upon this rock I will build my church, and the gates of hell shall not prevail against it. And I will give to thee the keys of the kingdom of heaven. And whatsoever thou shalt bind upon Earth, it shall be bound also in heaven; and whatsoever thou shalt loose upon Earth, it shall be loosed also in heaven." (Matthew 16: 18,19). Thus St. Peter became the first Bishop of Rome or Pope, first called "Father,", then "Papa," and finally "Pope." The Pope in the Vatican, Rome, is the earthly head of the Roman Catholic Church. Roman priests are directly descended from the first twelve apostles through the Pope, the Cardinals, and the Bishops, by a consecration ritual called "The Laying On of Hands." Roman Catholic priests live in celibacy, that is, they do not marry.

Roman Catholics believe in seven sacraments, which are formal outward acts that symbolize the inward spiritual receiving of grace (divine assistance) from God. These sacraments are: Baptism, in which babies or sometimes adults become Christians; Holy Eucharist, to reenact

The Cross, symbol of Christianity.

the Last Supper of bread and wine first celebrated by
Jesus Christ with his apostles before his death; Confirmation, by which a young person becomes a responsible
adult member of the church; Holy Matrimony; Penance,
which consists of confession of sins, contrition, penance
and absolution; Holy Orders, by which a person becomes
a priest; and Extreme Unction, to receive a final blessing
before death.

Roman Catholics attend Mass every Sunday and Holy Day of Obligation, according to the church calendar, and follow the Ten Commandments of the Old Testament plus Christ's teachings. One can recognize a Catholic Church because every church has a cross on its steeple, dome or campanile, which is a bell tower.

At the entrance to a Roman Catholic church, there is a fount of holy water. Catholics dip their fingers into the water and make a sign of the cross, touching the forehead, the chest, the left and right shoulders. This is a reminder that Christ died on the cross to redeem the souls of all people. The water that is used has been blessed by a priest and salt has been added as a symbol of everlasting life. And so Catholics purify themselves symbolically before coming into the church, following a practise that is followed in many other religions.

Next they genuflect (kneel and make the sign of the cross) before the altar because it is the place where priests keep the bread and wine of the Holy Eucharist that have been already consecrated. The blessed Host bread and wine represent the presence of God, so the altar is a holy place. Statues remind them of the saints who lived exemplary lives, but the statues themselves are not worshipped. Anyone can light votive candles in a special place near the altar and pray for a special intention or in memory of someone in particular.

On the walls are fourteen stations of the cross, which represent fourteen phases of the walk Jesus made carrying the cross along the Via Dolorosa (the Way of Sorrow) on his way to Golgotha where he was executed. People sometimes say particular prayers in front of each station of the cross.

A rosary is often used by Catholics to help them pray. The rosary is a string of fifty-five or fifty-nine beads and a small crucifix; it was first used about the tenth century. Using beads for concentration in worship is a method used in many religions. As Catholics pray with the rosary, they finger the beads and meditate on the fifteen mysteries of the life of Jesus and his family, starting with the Annunciation of his birth.

The emphasis of the Roman Catholic religion is on Jesus' teachings, his redemption of man by his death on the cross, and the fact that God loves all people alike, both good and bad.

The Eastern Orthodox Catholic Church

Members of the Eastern Orthodox branch of the Catholic Church believe that it is the real heir of the apostolic succession and that the Western Roman Church, along with later Protestant groups, deviated from the true church which is theirs.

After moving toward separation for many centuries, the final break away from the Roman Catholic Church was effected by the Eastern Orthodox Catholic Church A.D. 1054. At this time, the Roman Church had resumed former disciplines with which the Eastern Church disagreed. These rules, such as fasting on Saturday, celibacy for priests, the separation of Baptism from Confirmation, were minor points in the differences; the major disagreements were more nebulous and though not so clearly defined, were accepted as irreconcilable.

The Eastern Orthodox Catholic Church, with about 161,774,350 members, emphasizes the mystical fellowship of its members in unity with Christ. The Church is not so much concerned with its organization and structure, as its being a sign of the unity of God and man, a bridge between Heaven and Earth. The visible church is its ritual; the invisible is the mystical Christ, with the Holy Spirit acting through the worshippers. Salvation is not possible alone; it is possible only in this unity of people in the church. Hermetic saints cannot be saved. Sin is individual, but salvation is unified.

Since Christ is the Eastern Church and acts through the Church, the Church is the final authority on Earth. It was always so, before the Bible, so the Bible is not the authority for the Eastern Church, nor is the Pope. The authority lies in the living organism of the Church with all its members, laymen and priests together. To the Church is revealed truth, not to one person at a time.

Like the Roman Church, the Eastern Orthodox Church recognizes the validity of the seven sacraments and emphasizes faith in the Incarnation and Resurrection of Christ.

The practical existence of the Eastern Church has been difficult. People of the Near East and the Balkans have had to live first under the pressure of Islamic control and then with no spiritual freedom allowed by their controlling governments.

In the former U.S.S.R., the Eastern Church was successively suppressed by the Mongols, the Teutonic Knights, the Polish and then the Lithuanian armies. After 1943, the Russian quietly commenced restoration of church structures destroyed under Communism with formation of patriarchs' councils. With the advent of glasnost in the '80s, the church in the former U.S.S.R. is once more being revitalized. In Greece, Serbia, Bulgaria and Rumania, the Greek Orthodox Eastern Catholic Church has endured throughout many trials, sometimes silently, sometimes more vocally. In the United States, the Greek Orthodox Church is found throughout all states of the country.

Protestants

Although all Christians were and continue to be united by their belief in Jesus Christ, there occurred in the fifteenth and sixteenth centuries many breaks away from the Catholic traditions by reformers called Protestants who disagreed with some of the church's practises and inter-pretations of scripture. This break-away period is referred to as The Reformation.

The time was right for Protestantism, the youngest of the three Christian traditions. In western Europe, and especially in Germany, there were ancient grudges between emperors and the Pope. The Reformation was an attempt to return the church to its original ways, from which it was believed by some European leaders that the Catholic Church had strayed.

The Humanists in the North opened fire on the monks of the monasteries, who, they said, were often lazy and ignorant. It was at this time that Erasmus, a Dutch Humanist, translated into Latin a correct version of the New Testament from its original Greek. He emphasized his zeal to share the Bible with everyone by prefacing his translation with these words:

"I could wish that every woman might read the Gospel and the Epistles of St. Paul. Would that these were translated into each and every language so that they might be read and understood not only by Scots and Irishmen, but also by Turks and Saracens... Would that the farmer might sing snatches of Scripture at his plough, that the weaver might hum phrases of Scripture to the tune of his shuttle, that the traveller might lighten with stories from Scripture the weariness of his journey."

A German monk named Martin Luther was upset by the Roman Church's selling of indulgences, which meant that sins could be forgiven by a donation of money to the church, and he published his Ninety-five Theses that protested this and other practises of the Church. For this, he was excommunicated from the Roman Church, and this was the beginning of what was to become the Lutheran Church, found today mostly in Scandinavia, Germany, and the United States. Lutheranism will be discussed in the chapter on Scandinavian religions, but its underlying principles are well worth repeating.

Lutherans stress the great love of God that should be reflected in people's love for each other. Faith in God and the correct interpretation of his Word is important. Liberty is respected and the importance of the sacraments is recognized.

Much beautiful music has come out of the Lutheran Church tradition. J.S. Bach was an outstanding composer of Lutheran sacred music that is played extensively today.

An extremely important figure during the Reformation was John Calvin. He was born a Frenchman on July 10, 1509, but he was exiled to Switzerland eventually because of his convictions. He, like Luther, wanted to see the Catholic Church return to its original ways by rejecting what he considered to be scholastic errors and papal heresies. An important facet of Calvinism has been belief in predestination, which means having faith that God continually guides those people who are destined for salvation i.e. eternal life. His preaching influenced the founding of many Protestant churches, among them the Presbyterian, the Reformed, the Congregational and the Baptist.

In England, the English church broke away from the Roman Church in 1534 when Henry VIII was king. He quarreled with the Pope of Rome who refused to grant his desired divorce, confiscated monastic property in England, gave some Protestant doctrines official sanction, and made himself head of the new Anglican Church. This church has retained many of the Catholic traditions and has been what T.S. Eliot called, "a mean between Papacy and Presbyter." The Anglican Church tries to combine the faith and sacraments of the apostolic Catholic Church with the necessary reasoning of the Reformation, especially Calvinism.

There have been many other manifestations of radical Protestantism, two hundred fifty in the United States alone. These smaller groups who broke away to practise their faith in their own way have been called "the step-children of the Reformation."

One category of radical Protestants is called Evangelical. The Evangelists seek to conform with the will of God as interpreted by them in their reading of the Scriptures. They believe in political involvement, the rights of man, and freedom. Among the Evangelicals are the Baptists, the Methodists, the Congregationalists and the Quakers.

Another facet of Protestantism is revealed in the Humanists' emphasis on the church's relationship to secular society. They seek to fit Christianity into prevailing cultural patterns, and see the church as a sociological unit. The Unitarian Church fits this pattern.

Protestants emphasize the supreme authority of the Bible, both the Old and New Testaments. They believe that the Holy Spirit was the inspiring force behind the writers who did the composition. The core of the Bible is the Gospel (good news). The Gospel refers to the story of God's kingdom, man's salvation, and the life of Christ. Protestants teach that Jesus is the head of the church and that the church is the agent of his will on Earth. Man reaches salvation by believing in Jesus, whose life, death and resurrection assured the believer's place in Heaven. Good deeds can't get one to Heaven; belief in Jesus and his sacrifice does.

In Jesus' manhood, Protestants believe that he set an example for people by the way he lived on Earth. They also believe that Jesus is with people today. "Lo, I am with you always, even unto the end of the world." (Matthew 28:20)

Protestants feel responsible for teaching others about Christ and for living exemplary lives of ethical behavior and charity for all.

The Mormons

In 1820-1830 in the United States, another deviation in the Christian Church occurred when Joseph Smith from Palmyra, New York, announced that he had been visited by the angel, Moroni, who gave him instructions leading to a new Gospel called The Book of Mormon. This Book formed the basis for the Church of Jesus Christ of Latter-Day Saints, also known as the Mormon Church.

The Book reveals that Jesus returned to Earth a second time after his first resurrection, this time appearing in South America. There he named twelve new apostles and gave them a choice whether to remain on Earth or to return to Heaven with him. Three chose to remain, and these three "Nephites" wander the world doing good deeds.

Because they were different, especially for their practise of polygamy, Mormons were often persecuted by other members of society. Joseph Smith and his brother, Hyrum, were eventually killed by a lynch mob in the Midwest. Before his death, Smith predicted that the Mormons would go to the West, and there they would find the twelve lost tribes of Israel. When Brigham Young assumed leadership of the church and led the Mormons to settle in Utah, the contacts and spiritual coexistence between them and the Indians there affirmed their belief that these Indians were indeed the twelve lost tribes. In 1890, polygamy was outlawed by the church to conform to state laws, but the practise still exists in isolated places today.

Mormonism is a vital and growing religion. Today there are seven and seven-tenths millions of Mormons, many of whom live in the western United States, but there are three and four-tenths million Mormons overseas, living mostly in Latin America, who have been converted by very active missionaries.

Because many Protestant and Catholic Churches have sent missionaries to all parts of the world, particularly during the 18th, 19th and 20th centuries, there are Christians in every remote area of the globe. Along with churches, missions have established innumerable schools, orphanages and hospitals.

Scandinavia

What we know about the early religions of Scandinavia, we have learned from pictographs, runes and skaldic poetry found in Norway, Sweden, Denmark, and other countries of Europe and in North America.

One discovery, the Kensington Stone, aroused much excitement when it was found in Minnesota in 1898 by a Swedish farmer named Olaf Oliman. The runes on this two hundred pound, partially buried stone recorded an Indian attack on a Norse landing party in the area in 1362. Since it is widely believed that early Norse sailors did indeed reach and explore North America, this stone was a much-desired verification of the theory. Careful examination however, led most scholars to conclude that the stone was probably a forgery engineered and promoted by Oliman until his death in 1935. The skeptics argued that of the twenty-eight runes on the stone, only fourteen of them even existed in the fourteenth century and, of the sixty-four words used, forty-five were recent or fictitious forms of Swedish or Danish/Norwegian combinations. The mysterious Kensington Stone remains in a museum in Alexandria, Minnesota.

The authentic rock carvings and paintings of the Arctic Stone Age that have been found in Norway, Sweden, Denmark, Finland, Iceland and Greenland reveal evidence of an early hunting culture dependent on reindeer, elk, bear, whales and fish for sustenance. The art illustrates the worship of gods of hunting who had the power to provide a bountiful supply of animals for food and shelter. With the progression of the culture to agriculture around 3000 B.C., the gods of the soil, rain and harvest became equally important to the people.

A War Culture

Following the invasion of the Indo-European Battle-Axe tribes from the south about 2000 B.C., there was no longer pictorial emphasis on the gods of nature. What became most important was the glory of battles, war ships, courage and male power. Warrior gods became most important in the culture. Precious stones decorated metallic shield-like discs which have been found like buried treasure in bogs and pools. It became a culture that revered war.

Although the earliest runes do not appear until the third century A.D., the ancient skaldic poetry of the bards tells us about the warrior gods. ''The Voluspa,'' also known as ''Sybil's Prophecy,'' is probably the best-known of these divine poems.

In skaldic poetry, one also learns about Odinn, the chief god of creation, magic and poetry, who could assume the form of an eagle, a serpent, a raven, a wolf or a horse. An ancient warrior's courage was rewarded after

Runes

death by his being taken to Vaholl, or Valhalla, Odinn's palace in the World of Joy, from which he would go forth every day to do battle, and to which he would return every evening to dine peacefully on stewed boar flesh. When a warrior died, his body was either cremated or buried, along with that of his horse, his servants, sometimes his wife, his dog, his wealth, and even his ship, if he had one. The legend of the brave warrior, Sigurd, slayer of Fafnir, the dragon, and the Valkyries, Odinn's handmaidens, is typical and has been made into a popular opera by Wagner. If the warrior were a king or prince who died bravely in battle, he often became an object of worship as a demigod.

There are many legends about Thor, son of Odinn and Joro, the Earth Goddess. Thor's symbol, the hammer, is often found in pictographs. He was the god of thunder and of lightning bolts, which form he frequently took as he battled evil giants and giantesses, trolls, and the serpent, Midgardsorm, who lies coiled around the Earth. There were many evil gods in skaldic poetry, like Loki, who missed no chance to cause trouble in the world.

Along with gods, there were lesser spirits, such as the guardian disir, who were feminine spirits; the alfar, who were the light and dark elves; the dwarfs; and other Earth spirits who lived in rocks and in the ground.

Temples were erected to honor these early Scandinavian gods, but people also worshipped in forest groves, bringing blood sacrifices of animals and men to sacred rocks, stones, groves and waterfalls. Some animal sacrificial rites included consuming the meat and thereby receiving power from the god invoked. Human sacrifices were usually criminals or slaves, but even kings were sacrificed in times of extreme distress.

Tollund Man is the name that has been given to the mummified remains of such a man that was discovered in 1948 in a peat bog at Tollund, Jutland. The body is remarkably preserved and dates from the Iron Age (400 B.C.- A.D. 400). About one hundred such specimens have been uncovered, and it is believed that these people were buried as sacrifices to various gods, perhaps voluntarily giving their lives.

The Vikings

During the ninth and tenth centuries, A.D., Catholic missionaries came to Scandinavia and converted many of the kings to Christianity. Those who resisted this growing influence of the Christians, as well as the seizing of their estates and the rise of the monarchies, left Scandinavia to become Vikings. They explored and settled in new lands to the North and West, particularly in Iceland. There they lived according to their old beliefs that courage in life and in battle was what was most important in a man. They earned a reputation for their fierce attacking and sacking of Western European cities for loot. Sometimes Vikings settled into the territories that they conquered. For example, in the year 911, the French king Charles III the

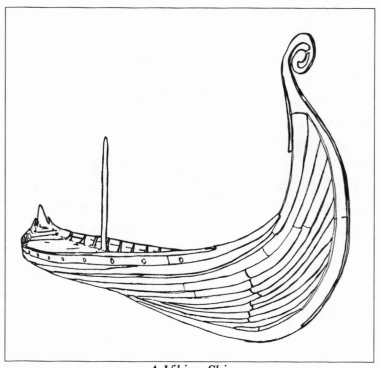

A Viking Ship

Simple accepted Rollo the Viking and his large band of
Northmen (Normans) as his vassels. Rollo and his men
were baptized Christians and became the French anteced-
ents of William the Conqueror who invaded England in
1066.

The Vikings used many spears, bows and arrows, but
the sword was generally their most prized possession.
These swords were often elaborately designed of gold and
silver. However, the symbol of the Vikings became the
Nordic long-handled battle-ax. Viking men wore long-
sleeved thick coats and trousers with long cloaks hanging

from their shoulders. For their battle costume they added shields, coats of mail, leather or iron helmets, and sometimes armlets for decoration. Their horses' saddles, spurs, and harnesses were richly decorated also. Their women often were dressed in costly fabrics acquired as loot, such as Chinese silk and gold brocade.

Because these Viking sea warriors achieved extraordinary success by their use of ships, they customarily buried their dead in ships under huge barrows. In the ships there were special chambers for the remains, tents, small boats, sledges, carts, and personal belongings. Some stone burial chambers that are shaped like boats have also been found throughout Scandinavia. Cremation was sometimes practised, but gradually it died out as Christianity eventually spread to include the Vikings.

The Lutherans

It was in the sixteenth century that a new form of Christianity from Germany became popular in the Scandinavian countries. The Lutheran Church had been started by a German Augustinian Roman Catholic monk named Martin Luther who was not trying to start a new church when he openly objected to some of the practises of the Roman Catholic Church. In 1521 Luther was excommunicated by the church for his theses of objections. His followers, against his will, became known as belonging to the Lutheran Church. It was after his death in 1546 that the Lutheran Church spread throughout most of Germany and Scandinavia. There it eventually became the national church of Norway, Sweden, Denmark, and Finland. Today, over ninety per cent of the populations of these countries are members of the Lutheran Church, part of the seventy-five million in the world.

Lutherans believe that a loving God offers grace and salvation if people will honor Him and Jesus Christ. They contend that the Bible teaches us this, and that through it, we can learn how to live moral lives. They follow Martin Luther's example in his objection to the concept of fear that prevailed in the Catholic Church of his time, the idea that one must love God or be punished. Instead of a terrible God, Luther taught of a benevolent Creator who manifested his love for mankind in the life, death, and resurrection of Jesus Christ.

Islam

The newest of the world's most popular monotheistic (of the doctrine that there is only one God) religions is Islam, which began in Saudi Arabia A.D. 610. Islam, with about 924,611,500 members today, is sometimes called Muhammadanism after its founder, the prophet Muhammad. Islam means "submission to God."

Seventh century Saudi Arabia was a land of Semites, many of them Jews, pagans who believed in many gods, and Christians. Muhammad, who was an uneducated, handsome, red-bearded camel driver until he married a wealthy widow, spent much time meditating in the desert. When he was about forty years old, the angel Gabriel appeared to him one day in a sandy desert cave. Gabriel said he would reveal to Muhammad how Allah wanted people to live in order to worship him, and how to reach final happiness for eternity. "Allah" is the Arabic word for "God." All that Allah revealed to Muhammad through Gabriel in his many visits to him became the basis for the Islam religion, 114 suras or chapters which make up the sacred book of Islam called the Qur'an (Koran).

As Muhammad followed the angel's instructions to teach the people of Mecca, the city where he lived, about Allah's revelations to him, he was believed by some, but given much trouble by the pagans, Jews, and others who hated and feared him. Therefore, it was A.D. 622 when he left with seventy followers and their families to settle in Medina, a city two hundred miles to the north. This Hijra (flight) and the ensuing battles to overcome Medina and later Mecca, made Muhammad the religious and political head of that part of the world and signalled the real beginning of Islam.

Islamic Beliefs

There were five main parts to the lessons given by Gabriel to Muhammad and then written into the Qur'an:
    1. The Shahada or Statement of Faith i.e. Allah is the one God, powerful but merciful, who created man to worship and serve him. Muhammad is the messenger of Allah.

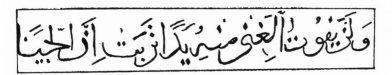

Writing from the Koran (Arabic)

2. There are angels to serve between Allah and man.

3, Allah will judge everyone on the last day and everyone will go to Paradise or Hell.

4. People should be generous in sharing their wealth.

5. Muhammad is Allah's prophet; there were many prophets before him, all of whom should be respected, like Abraham, Noah, Moses, Jesus Christ, and others.

In order to achieve salvation, Muslims must do the following:

1. Worship Allah by reciting the Shahada daily and by praying the "salat" five times facing Mecca (formerly Jerusalem), alone or with others. The appointed muezzin, dressed in loose black robe and green turban, calls the people to prayer from a high tower that has a circular platform and is called a minaret.

2. Give alms to the poor.

3. Fast during the daylight hours of the month of Ramadan, for discipline and thanksgiving, recognizing that Allah will provide for you.

4. Make a pilgrimage to the holy city of Mecca in Hejaz, Saudi Arabia, once during your lifetime.

In Mecca there is, in addition to the birthplace of Muhammad, the Ka'ba, the sacred altar built by Abraham and Ishmael, his son by Hagar the concubine, for the worship of God. The Ka'ba is a cube-like building enclosed by a huge wall and surrounded by seven minarets. Enshrined in the Ka'ba is the Black Stone. Seven inches in diameter, it is oval in shape and a mysterious object of superstitious worship. Legend says that it was once pure white and had been given to Abraham by Gabriel; later it turned black because of the sins of men.

The four major rules for salvation, plus hundreds of others which cover all phases of Muslim life, make up the Shari'a, the Law of Islam. They are all based on the Qur'an and the Hadith, which was written later by Muslim teachers to tell the story of Muhammad's life. Some other very important rules of Islam are that you do not steal, lie, speak evil of anyone, indulge in intoxication, eat pork, gamble, worship idols, commit adultery or break your word.

Friday is the Islamic Sabbath. On the Sabbath a Moslem goes to the mosque for a service. In the outer room of the mosque he removes his shoes in order to pay respect to the house of Allah and to the other worshippers. Then he goes into a room where there are basins of water in which to wash his hands, face, feet and any other unclean body parts.

Symbol of the Muslim Faith

Purified, he enters the prayer room with a clean body and a clean heart, for now he tries to fill his head with only good and positive thoughts. The floor of the mosque rooms are covered with lovely prayer rugs on which the worshippers kneel to pray. In the prayer room, there may be floral or geometric designs on the wall, but there are no pews, chairs, idols, statues or musical instruments. Usually there are only men present, for the Prophet Mohammed was supposed to have said that it was better for a woman to pray in her own house or courtyard. However, there are sometimes services with, and for, women. The Muslim bows his head to the floor as he prays. Then he listens to a sermon by the imam or minister.

It was said of Mohammed's habits that he divided his day into three portions. The first portion he gave to Allah, the second to his family, and the third to his people. He loved freedom so he freed all his personal slaves. He believed in the equality of people so he gave away any

149

jewels that were given to him by his followers.

Sometimes there is criticism of the Muslim custom of polygamy in some of its branches. Practising Muslims cite the life of Mohammed as their example. Actually, Mohammed lived happily for thirty years with his wife until she died. It was only then that he installed a harem of nine wives with whom he lived quietly and peacefully for seven years until his death.

Some Muslim women today appear in public only when completely covered except for the eyes, a custom called "purdah." The Koran does not specify that this is necessary, but it became part of some Muslims' tradition. In other traditions, the women wear veils across their faces when appearing in public.

In an Islamic marriage, the partners are asked to declare in public and in front of two witnesses that the marriage is of their own free will; this creates a civil contract. Then there follows a religious ceremony with or without an imam officiating. Held in the bride's home with friends and relatives in attendance, there are readings from the Koran, prayers and a brief wedding ceremony with or without a ring. The father of the bride gives her away along with a dowry.

A Muslim funeral is supposed to be simple and dignified. The body is washed, perfumed and wrapped in a white cloth seamless shroud. After a service of prayers, the coffin of the dead is carried on the shoulders of friends to the grave site. Mourners follow in procession and it is believed that Gabriel, Angel of Revelation;

Michael, Angel of Rain; Azrail, Angel of Death; and Israfil, Angel of Resurrection, walk with those who mourn. Muslims believe in the mystery of the resurrection, that both body and soul will some day be raised up and renewed.

Islam After Muhammed

It was A.D. 630 when Mohammed led the raid on Mecca and conquered it for Islam. When he died in 632, he is said to have died whispering, "Gabriel, come close to me." Aisha, his favorite wife, said that the angel had come to lead Mohammed to the life beyond.

After Mohammed's death, he was succeeded by Abu Bakr, who became the first Khalifa, deputy of Mohammed and leader of Islam. In order to keep peace with his followers, who had always lived as nomadic tribes that raided their neighbors territories for booty, Abu began to lead such raids on nearby countries and thereby spread the word of Islam.

First the Muslim army took over Syria, Iraq and Egypt, where they had no trouble winning because the armies of the Byzantine and Persian Empires were exhausted after fifty years of war.

Next they moved into Persia, Afghanistan and what is now Pakistan, across North Africa to Gibraltar and Spain and the south of France, where they were finally stopped in the Battle of Tours A.D. 732.

The Taj Mahal at Agra
Built (1632-54) by Mogul Emperor Shah Jahan
as a mausoleum for his beloved wife, Mumtaz.
An example of Islamic architecture in India

It wasn't until 1492, however, that the Muslims were completely ejected from Europe by the Spanish Inquisition, when the Roman Catholic Church became very powerful in Spain.

Wherever they went to spread word of their faith, the Muslims recognized and spared those minorities who believed in one God as they did; these were the Jews, the Christians, and the Zoroastrians.

They continued to take their lessons of Islam into East and West Africa, Malaysia, Indonesia, the Philippines and Eastern China, via trading caravans and ships. Finally they penetrated India, where they reached their greatest power under the Mogul emperors from A.D. 1556 to 1707.

In India, it was a challenge to the Muslims because most Indians were Hindu and remained Hindu. Bloody religious wars were continually waged between the Indian Hindus and the Moslems. The disputes were extremely violent and were not settled until 1947 when, through the efforts of the United Nations, part of India was designated as a separate country for Muslims; this new country was called Pakistan.

Islam Today

Islam differs from most other religions in that the religious and political lives of the people are not separated. When Islamic law conflicts with political law, compromises are made for civil harmony, but Muslim families adhere to the Islamic code in their homes.

There are two principle divisions in Islam: the Sunni and the Shi'a or Shi'ite. Ninety percent of all Muslims are Sunni. They are Orthodox Moslems who stress the need for an inner moral spiritual life in accordance with Mohammed's teachings. The other ten percent are the Shi'a, within which category there are more subdivisions.

One of these divisions, the Imamis or Twelvers who predominate in Iran, Pakistan, Iraq and southern Lebanon, as well as in Turkey, believe in the final authority of the imams (teachers) of Islam, the first of whom after Mohammed was Ali, his cousin. To the Islamic Creed, "There is no God but Allah and Mohammed is his apostle," they add, "and Ali is his waliy (comrade)". The Imamis' descendants are the ayatollahs who have the power to make rulings on, and to interpret, the Shari'a their way. Problems occur when the interpreted laws of the Shi'ites conflict with international understanding of right and wrong.

For example, a Shi'ite can enter into a temporary marriage of a day, a week or a year. He can conceal his faith in what he considers a hostile society and is not considered to be guilty of hypocrisy or lying. This is in contrast to many other faiths in which martyrs have shown a willingness to die rather than conceal or deny their religious beliefs. A Muslim who wants to leave his faith can legally be put to death; other faiths allow you to choose.

A Shi'ite who steals may have his hands cut off, and a married Shi'ite who is unfaithful may be stoned to death. These radical punishments are difficult for non-Shi'ites to recognize and accept in an age that stresses certain universal basic human rights.

Various interpretations of the Koran have led to the formation of the Hadith or Tradition in ways that are sometimes conflicting as to the intent of what Mohammed transcribed to be the law. For example, the "Jihad" means "exerting one's power to repel the enemy, whether the enemy be a declared visible enemy who attacks you, the devil who causes you to do evil, or yourself, the parts of you that are selfish and cruel." "Jihad" has been interpreted by some branches of Muhammadanism as meaning "war; the spreading of Islam by force." This is debateable because the Qur'an specifically states that Allah does not want his religion spread by compulsion or force. The Koran stresses that Muslims should always be aware of others' inclination toward peace and follow them, while trusting in Allah to protect them from treachery. The Prophet did promise, however, that those who fell facing the enemy will go directly to Heaven.

The varied interpretations have made it extremely difficult for other nations to understand the Shi'ites, especially of Iran, who seem to harbor an uncompromising unwillingness to tolerate other cultures peacefully. Because the religious leaders are also the political leaders of Iran, they exert a great deal of power over their people and are often at odds with other countries' political leaders.

Native Americans lived in harmony with all the facets of nature.

The New World

North America

When European explorers of the fifteenth and sixteenth centuries were looking for a new route to India and China, they discovered North America and its Indian cultures that had been developing simultaneously with theirs.

The next wave of newcomers in the seventeenth century consisted of refugees from religious persecution. Strangely enough, these former victims showed very little understanding or tolerance for Native American ways. On the contrary, they did all they could to scatter and eventually subdue them. They seemed to have little desire to coexist with Indian traditions which were simpler and closer to nature than the European ways that had caused them to leave their former homes.

The North American Indian's religion reflected his method for survival. Expressions varied from the animal-dependent tribes of the North, which extended from Alaska through Canada and the northern continental United States, to the horticultural tribes of the South. Survival and religion revolved around living in harmony with, and with respect for, nature.

The Northern tribes depended entirely for food and shelter on products of hunting, along with fishing and natural food gathering. Therefore they identified very closely with animals.

Since names were an extremely important part of their culture, Native Americans often named their children after an animal or a bird that was respected for its courage, beauty, strength or speed.

Whole tribes, clans, and men's secret societies, especially among the Ojibwas, would adopt for their guardian spirit a particular animal who would be their protector. This guardian spirit was known as a totem. In return for guardianship, the tribe would never kill, injure or eat the particular animal. This practise of totemism was prevalent in tribes of North, Central and South America. Totem poles have been found which symbolize the spirits. Some of the popular animal spirits were the bear, the coyote and the raven; the jaguar and the monkey were especially popular totem animals in South America.

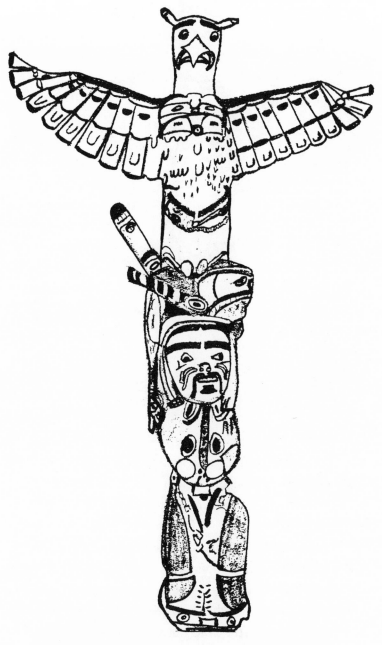

Thunderbird and Whale totem of the Kwakiutls
(SW Canada, NW U.S.)

Mythological creatures were also a part of the culture. The thunderbird of the Southwest is often depicted in
Indian art as the cause of thunder and lightning. The
Indians of the plains believed that the Earth rests on the
back of a giant turtle.

Besides animal spirits, the Indians believed in spirits
of trees, plants, rocks, mountains (especially volcanoes),
wind, rain and all facets of Nature. Some tribes would not
plow the earth because they considered the Earth their
mother goddess and they did not want to hurt her. The
farming tribes of the Southwest prayed to their goddess of
the corn, their staple crop, for fertility and a bountiful
harvest.

One popular belief among the Indians was that a sacred tree held up the heavens, the home of a Supreme Being, often symbolized by an eagle. This wise and powerful old god was eminent, but more remote than the God of Western non-Indian traditions. Appeals in the form of prayer or sacrifice were made to this god only under critical circumstances. He usually was not depicted as having created men.

Legends relate that men came to live on Earth through the efforts of some culture hero, often depicted as an animal. One tale credits the spider for men's creation, because spiders can made something out of nothing. Another tale relates how the union of the Sky Father and the Earth Mother resulted in the birth of men. Other myths describe how men ascended from a spirit world in the center of the Earth.

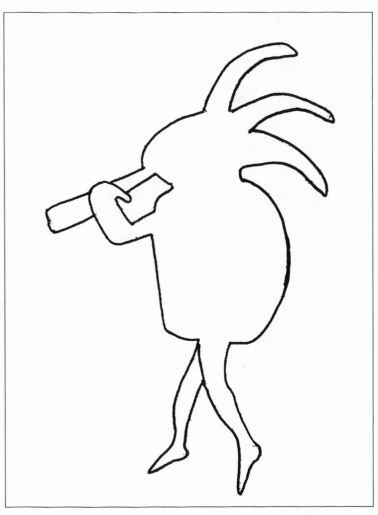

"Kokopelli is not only the flowing tones of a flute in the desert, but a metaphor for listening to some mysterious and creative part of ourselves. It is the desert earth spirit alive today in the form of creative human ability."
David Aguirre.

A favorite legend of the southwestern horticultural Indians is about Kokopelli. The story of Kokopelli, a humpbacked flute playing spirit, is thought to have originated in Arizona and New Mexico between 1050 and 1200. He is often pictured in petroglyphs and on pottery, leading early man into the world from the center of the Earth. With his flute he provided the warmth of music; in his hump he carried the seeds for the plants of the world.

Sometimes the underworld of the Indian cosmos was considered to be the abode of wicked gods, usually symbolized by the snake.

The gods manifested themselves in many voices: the thunder and lightning, the winds, and the roar of moving water in the surf, streams and waterfalls. Rainbows were the glorious clothes of the gods.

Because the entire universe was controlled by them, there was little sacrifice to the gods practised among North American Indians. It was as if you couldn't offer to give to the spirits anything more than what they already possessed.

The Medicine Man

Along with reverence for the gods and the chief of their tribe, the Indians paid most respect to their tribe's medicine man or woman. Called a shaman, orenda, wakan man or wakanda, he either inherited his power, was called to the position by spirits, or was chosen by a special council of the tribe. Usually he would take instruction from the retiring medicine man who would indicate the transfer of power by ceremonially spitting tobacco juice into the mouth of the new wakanda. Participation in the ceremony signalled the acceptance of responsibility for tribal teaching and leading in rituals.

One of the shaman's most important functions was to conjure up dreams or visions to predict the future. Tobacco smoke, magic, narcotics, peyote, mushrooms, self-torture, and fasting were used to induce apparitions. Transvestites and homosexuals often became medicine men because of their unusual relationship with both sexes.

Although another member of the tribe, called the wise man, usually did the doctoring with herbs and surgery, the shaman used visions to diagnose illnesses. Disease was believed to be caused by enchantment, ancestral sins, intrusion of a foreign object in cases of injury like a broken bone, broken taboos or, in the case of mental illness, the loss of one's soul.

The wakanda sometimes used a sucking straw inserted into an incision in order to extract a disease from a patient's body. This practise led to pipe smoking of tobacco for pleasure.

The pipe was also used as a fetish representing a link between a man and his guardian spirit. A fetish is any object believed to have magical power to protect or aid its owner. Other objects used as fetishes by the Indians were stone figures, sacred poles, arrows, hats and wheels.

Another important visible sign of the guardian spirit

of a tribe was the medicine bundle. The medicine bundles varied in content, but usually contained some animal parts of the totem animal, rattles, pipes and/or corncobs. The bundle was sacred and was opened only to be displayed during ceremonies. At that time, the shaman himself would be decorated with feathers, fur, claws and/or the skin of the totem spirit as he performed his ritual dance or ceremony. In the Eastern Iroquois tribes, the medicine man usually wore a wooden mask also.

Ceremonies were usually performed before Indian braves left the village to do battle or to hunt. The rituals were also used to influence winds and rain, to cure disease and to request or to thank the spirits for fertility and bountiful harvests. Whole tribes participated in seasonal festival dances for crops, health and puberty rites. Before these dances, every participant would purify himself in a sweat sauna and by drinking "black tea" to induce vomiting for inner cleansing. Within the tribes, there were sometimes secret societies of men who held their own rituals, prayers and dances.

The Indians believed that man had two souls: one soul of conscious life and movement, the other soul free to leave the sleeping body to wander, sometimes as far as to the Land of the Dead. One of the shaman's duties was to send his own free soul to the Land of the Dead to rescue other free souls who had gone and were in danger of being trapped there forever. The Milky Way and the rainbow were two paths to the Land of the Dead. Some clans believed in possible return from there as in reincar-

Medicine Woman with rattles during an incantation (N.A.)

nation. The Land of the Dead was not a place of punishment; evildoers could not go there, but had to roam the Earth forever as ghosts or go elsewhere.

Care of the body after death varied among tribes. Some Indians erected platforms on which the remains rested, exposed to vultures, after which the bones were buried. Others cremated the body or buried it in the earth. The deceased were often prayed to and asked for help. The Kachina dances of the Southwestern tribes were performed especially to ask departed spirits of ancestors for help with rain and fertility.

Spirits of all kinds permeated Indian life. They were not remote, except for the Great Spirit, but lived among the people on Earth where particular places were considered their sacred abodes. Water places were especially sacred: lakes, rivers, seas, hot springs and waterfalls. Mountains and volcanoes provided spirit homes, as did the underground places from which earthquakes evolved. Native Americans lived in harmony with all these spirits by respecting them and all the facets of nature.

Today there are one and a half million North American Indians, half of whom live on reservations. Although remnants of the old ways of coexisting with Nature endure among the older Indians, most of the cultural patterns of peaceful Native Americans have been destroyed by the white man's exploitation of them and their land.

Indian Cults

In response to the takeover of their territories by the white man, a variety of Indian cults developed from the eighteenth century to the present. There were two phases to this development. The early phase was centered around Indian hostility to the invaders, and promised salvation in the form of a return to the old ways. As the Indians lost control of the land because of the superior weapons, broken treaties, and large numbers of settlers backed by the army, cults were formed which recommended adapting to the white man's ways, while maintaining some measure of independence and retaining of ancient traditions.

The first cults included the Ghost Dancers of the plains Indians and the Paviotsos of Nevada and California. Ghost Dancers were so named because the dancers invoked the spirits of their ancestors to help in the regeneration of the world and the return of the Indians to the old ways. Along with prayers to the dead, fasting and stream bathing were part of the dance ritual. Performed initially for healing purposes, the dances became an expression of the complete rejection of the white man's ways. But this rejection was peaceful, and tribal prophets such as Wovoka and Wodziwob stressed the importance of tribal unity expressed in love and moral goodness toward each other, as well as the necessity of fighting only when they were forced to do so, and then with bows and arrows in their own way, not with guns.

Smoholla was a respected Indian prophet who belonged to the tribe of Dreamers of the Columbia River area of Washington and Oregon. After nearly dying and recovering, Smoholla taught his people by self-induced trances, wherein he would receive instructions from the spirits on how to live in the new world of the white man. It was he who taught that the white man's farming tools were evil, in that they caused pain to the Mother Earth when they were used to cultivate the land.

Two other of the many Western Indian cults were the Earth Lodge and the Bole Maru of California and Oregon. These were chiefly healing cults. The Bole Maru believed in one God, the devil, and eternal life in heaven or hell. There is evidence that it was the missionaries to the Indians who brought about such incorporation of the white man's church into the Indians' religion to form new syncretistic rituals.

The Shaker Cult of Puget Sound, Washington, rejected the Bible but accepted most of Catholicism and the teachings of Christ. This cult, which is still active, was named ''Shakers'' because of the participants' bodies actually shaking during times of celebrating religious ceremonies with fervor.

In the East, the cult of Canioda'yo (Handsome Lake), a Seneca of New York State, was influenced by its neighbors, the gentle Quakers. This cult combined the animistic worship and traditions of the Great Spirit and the lesser spirits, with the basic Quaker tenets that stressed fidelity and the value of silent prayer.

The largest American Indian cult became known as the Peyote Cult, named after a carrot-shaped cactus plant which produces unique psycho-physiological effects when eaten. It is not a narcotic since it is neither harmful nor habit-forming. In the religious practise, peyote is either drunk in tea or consumed at the end of the sacred "tipi" ceremony of prayers and meditation.

The Peyote Cult originated south of the Rio Grande and spread northward around the turn of this century. Used initially to cure alcoholism, tuberculosis and other illnesses, or to provide relief from hunger and fatigue, peyote was also used by Indian prophets like John Wilson of Oklahoma to induce visions for enlightenment.

The Peyote religion is based on elements of high morals, taken partly from Christianity. Members believe that the herbs mentioned in the Bible are peyote cacti; Baptism is performed with peyote tea instead of water. The religion teaches peaceful acceptance of the white man's conditions, but stresses the importance of independent Indian practises through the peyote sacramental ritual that belongs exclusively to the Indians. God is eminent to the Peyotes and they believe in the judgement and the kingdom of a loving and merciful God.

The Peyote Cult has long been the subject of controversy in the United States. Accusations of drug abuse in this century have made it difficult for these religious and peaceful Indians to practise their faith. There are over 200,000 members of the Peyote Cult living in an area that extends from the Great Lakes southward to the Rio Grande River.

South and Central America

When the Spaniards arrived in South America in the sixteenth century seeking land and gold for their king and church, they found the Indian tribes living there suppressed and governed by powerful priest-kings aided by a strong warrior class. Men like Cortez in Mexico, Pizzaro in Peru, and Valdivia in Chile, easily overthrew these governments with their superior military power and the Indian tribes reverted back to the former folk religions of their ancestors, while also responding to the influence of the Spanish Catholic missionaries.

A variety of artifacts in South America have led historians to make some interesting conclusions about the origins of the early South Americans and their religions. Evidence found in Equador and other Andean countries, dating from 3000 to 1500 B.C., suggests that the population originally arrived in that area by means of boats from southeast Asia. Identical ceramic artifacts have been discovered in the Andes and in southern Japan. These artifacts reflect the worship of a Mother Earth goddess. Evidence of Buddhist and Hindu cultures has been uncovered in Mexico, while ancient Chinese calendar gods have shown up in other parts of Central America!

Archeologists seem to agree that animism was the dominant religious practise in early South and Central America. Animal spirit worship, totemism emphasizing the jaguar, the tapir and the bat as guardian spirits were mingled with adoration of gods and goddesses, especially

Stone figure of Chalchihuitlicue, beautiful goddess of the waters of life, worshipped by ancient Mayans and Aztecs in Mexico.

those related to fertility and the harvest.

In the sixth century, B.C., concurrent with much

religious activity in the Middle and Far East, there seems to have occurred in South America a strong growth of religious organization, art, architecture and science. Throughout the thousand years before Christ, temples, altars and great cities were being built in South and Central America, the ruins of which exist today.

Math and astronomy were evidently very important to the religious organization. The heavens were the focus of both scientific study and worship of many celestial gods, of which the sun god was the most powerful. Human sacrifices were made to please these awesome gods. It was a time of many battles being fought among city tribes and those tribes who migrated from area to area; some tribes were overcome completely, taken into slavery and disappeared forever.

In Mexico, the Toltec Indians worshipped many gods, including the popular and much-pictured Quetzacoatl, "the feathered snake," who was the guardian of priests. About the fourteenth century, the Aztec Indians migrated southward from midwestern North America to Mexico and overcame the Toltecs. Legend says that they were led to the valleys of Mexico by Huitzilopochtle, the Aztec sun god, in 1325. In a vision, the god told the priests to find the place "where the eagle devours the horned snake." Following this advice, they settled in Tenochtitlan City, which is Mexico City today.

The Aztecs were skilled engineers and city planners, as well as brilliant military and political organizers. They

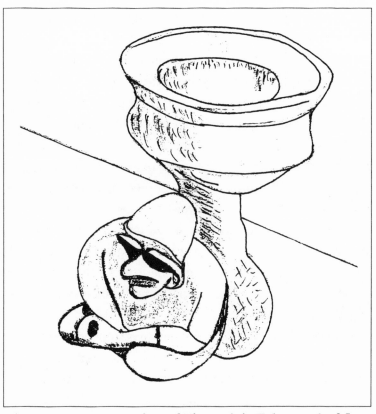

*A pottery representation of Xiutecuhti, Toltec god of fire,
Ruler of the Calendar, Lord of the Pole Star.*

formed a military dictatorship consisting of a hierarchy of
priest/king, priests and warriors. There was also a snake
woman, who was really a man and supervisor of the
temples and the priests. There was extensive use of narcotics and peyote in their rituals, and it was during this
period that human blood sacrifices became very important.

Although the Aztec king was reputedly compassionate toward his own people, there was constant warfare against neighboring tribes in order to provide enough human blood sacrifice victims for their gods. As many as 50,000 captives would be sacrificed each year; one ceremony alone saw the slaughter of 20,000 people! The priests and altars would be drenched in blood as the victims were slain, their beating hearts extracted and eaten by the participants. If the victim were a captured chief or brave warrior, he would be chained to a rock and given a wooden sword with a feather blade with which to fight for his freedom against five of the king's best warriors.

When Cortez expressed his shock at seeing the altar steps dripping with blood from sacrifices, Montezuma, who was the last of the Aztec kings, explained their conviction that the cosmos would be destroyed if they did not sacrifice this way. Aztecs also believed that one's fate after death was predetermined anyway by one's social class. Upper class people were destined to go to Paradise, and the underworld of Mictlan was the ultimate destination of commoners.

The overthrow of the Aztec culture by the Spaniards resulted in the people's return to their animistic religious beliefs. This was gradually altered by the increasing influence of the Catholic Spanish missionaries who had accompanied the conquering armies. The strongest church in South and Central America today remains the Roman Catholic Church.

Wherever indigenous people have been oppressed by invaders who controlled them politically, they have sought to find salvation and escape through their own unique religions.

Religions of Oppression

Throughout the world of the sixteenth through the twentieth centuries, religious sects have evolved among those people who are the victims of oppression. Imperialism and colonialism by European countries, especially in Africa, initiated contacts between native cultures, usually black, and more sophisticated cultures, usually white. Christian missionaries and Muslims traveled extensively in their efforts to spread word of their respective faiths and to proselytize the inhabitants.

As the invaders assumed control of their lands, natives were often victims of the class conflict resulting from the racial discrimination and ethnocentrism of the white landowners The resulting xenophobia of the natives and their resentment of unfair treatment led to the initial formation of religious groups that were openly hostile to the white colonists. Native prophets in Africa, as well as in Central and South America, preached a popular message that advocated ejection of the imperialists, a return to the old ways, and the seeking of a messiah to free them from the tyranny of the invaders.

In the beginning the new sects generally held onto the folk religious practises they had learned as part of their heritage. These ancient traditions of the natives were basically animistic in that they gave life to nature and natural objects. For example, the Bushmen of Southwest Africa not only prayed to a Supreme Being, but also to the moon and other celestial spirits for health and an abundant food supply for their desert families. The Bantus worshipped their ancestors along with the many gods of nature for whom they often kept sacred fires burning. Many tribes practised magic and commonly wore amulets for protection from evil spirits.

Later cults borrowed from the religious teachings of the missionaries, combined their rites with the old ways, and formed half-pagan, half-Christian, sometimes half-Muslim religions. Although the destruction of native cultural patterns and dispossession of tribal chiefs by the white man caused tribal members to seek a messiah to restore to them a social order of their own, Jesus Christ and Muhammad were not accepted by them as their messiahs. African leaders, such as Shabala, a Bantu, said that black men should have their own savior, uniquely coming only to them.

However, many groups did embrace some of the elements of Christianity. The Bible was often used to teach religion and the cross was sometimes used as an amulet i.e. "...in the name of the Father, Simon Kimbangu and Andre Matswa (two African sect leaders)."

The racism of the white men, even the missionaries, made the natives distrust and fear them. The introduction of money and subsequent greed for it added to the problems. Secret societies of rebellion formed to fight the white man's influence. In the Congo of the early 1900s, a respected native miracle worker named Epikilipikili established a pattern of peaceful rebellion against white colonials by refusing to pay taxes or to buy salt, which had been monopolized by the invaders for their profit. This political rebellion became a major religious movement that spread quickly among the native tribes of the area and successfully brought about some benefits for the native people.

In the 1900s, some African sects became affiliated with American Negro churches . Members resisted the work of missionaries, while preaching for a return to Africa of all black people whose ancestors had been sold abroad into slavery. Some sects chose to embrace Christianity or Islam entirely, all forswore the ancient black magic practises, and most of them developed into a blend of pagan and monotheistic religions.

In the Caribbean area in 1930, a black man named Marcus Garvey advocated a return to Ethiopia for all Negroes, where Emperor Haile Selassie would be their God. Ethiopia was then the only African country not colonized and controlled by white invaders. Garvey started the Ras Tafari, a cult which was based on the belief that the Negroes of Jamaica were members of the twelve lost tribes of Israel. Members accepted a Supreme Being, but no messiah, visions, missionaries or policemen! Today most Jamaican natives are anti-Western Christians, but there exists also some revival of African animistic religious practises.

Voodoo

In the former French colony of Haiti, the religion of Voodoo developed in the eighteenth century as a reaction to the cruelty of French Christian colonists who forced baptism onto the natives. While obliged to accept Christianity as their religion, the natives secretly worshipped their animistic spirits and continued to carry and believe in their fetishes. Makandal, an African Muslim from Santo Domingo, is called the Father of Voodoo. He was burned at the stake as a heretic by local authorities in 1758, after which he became known as Father Loa, a Voodoo saint.

Developed by slaves, Voodoo is an amalgam of features of African religions, especially those of

Dahomey; West Indian cult practises; and Roman Catholic liturgy, vestments and sacraments. Parallel religions that evolved about the same time are Santeria in Cuba, Obeah in Jamaica and Orisha in Brazil.

Members worship Loa, which are divine beings, sometimes deified ancestors, and comparable to the saints of the Roman Catholic Church. Each Loa has its color to be used in ritual, its own day of the week, its songs, prayers, sacred emblem to be drawn on the ground during the ceremony, and its unique behavior during possession.

Led by priest/leaders called "hungan" if male, "mambo" if female, members take part in public ceremonies, usually at night, that include prayers to their Loas and collective dancing. Ultimately a Loa is supposed to take possession of a subject and act through him in dancing, feasting or partaking in animal sacrifice (often a chicken or a goat). The subject is in a trance-like state while he and other participants dance until exhausted.

There are also secret ceremonies in Voodoo that include the use of magic and sorcery, curse charms, the creation of zombies, and belief in bloodsucking werewolves from whom your Loa will protect you.

Many other religious sects have been started in rebellion against colonial rulers in South America, Asia, Melanesia and Indonesia. Wherever indigenous people have been oppressed by invaders who controlled them politically, they have sought to find salvation and escape through their own unique religions.

19

Conclusion

Carl Jung, a Swiss psychologist who died in 1961, described religions as "therapies for the sorrows and disorders of the soul." We've discussed only a few of these "therapies," mostly the ones that have attracted the greatest number of people. But throughout history, there have been a myriad of small splinter groups of people who have elected to follow and adhere to their unique set of beliefs. The last two centuries in particular have given rise to hundreds of such communities.

There are some commune-centered sects like the Hutterites, Shakers and Amish Mennonites whose philosophies revolve around a mutually sharing community that stays detached from the mores of contemporary society as much as possible. Members live an unsophisticated life style that eschews pop culture and stresses piety and old-fashioned virtues.

There are messianic cults that are centered around one messiah, an individual who claims to be God incarnate or his spokesman. Television evangelists like Oral Roberts and Jim Bakker have had the loving support of thousands of twentieth-century Americans. A man named George Baker, alias Father Divine, had hundreds of thousands of Americans of the 1930s, most of them black, believing in his immortality until he died and wasn't resurrected.

Another group is the Millennialists, whose leaders predict the imminent end of the world as it is and the advent of Christ's reign on Earth. They instruct people on how to prepare for it by their evangelistic distribution of literature. There are over a million Jehovah's Witnesses in two hundred countries, members of the Millennialist church started in Pittsburgh, Pennsylvania, in 1872 by C.T.Russell under the name of the International Bible Students' Association. In 1931 Judge J.F. Rutherford sought to reaffirm the term ''Jehovah'' which was actually a misinterpretation in the Middle Ages of the name of God as written in Hebrew scripture, i.e. Yahweh. Rutherford said that those who took this name for their witness were God's privileged followers.

The religion of Jehovah's Witnesses is based on their interpretation of the Apocalyptic books of the Bible, especially "Daniel" and "The Book Revelation." The Apocalypse is the predicted time when God will destroy evil and raise up certain properly-living people to live in his perfect kingdom. Jehovah's Witnesses regard political divisions as tools of Satan and refuse to vote, serve in the military or salute the flag.

Then there are the Existentialists who encompass a wide range of people whose philosophy is that one's existence in a universe that is unexplainable is to be defined personally by each individual's own interpretation of good and bad, right and wrong. Some famous spokesmen for this philosophy have been Heidegger, Neitzsche, Sartre and Camus.

This philosophy is manifested in liberal churches like the Unitarian Church that issue no official statement of doctrine, but rather stress the personal exercise of judgement in matters of faith and morals. Born out of the study of the Bible in the Reformation and Post-Reformation periods, Unitarianism originally evolved out of some people's rejection of the Christian concept of the Trinity. The Trinity was the God of three parts, Father, Son and Holy Spirit. Michael Servetus was burned at the stake as a heretic in Switzerland in 1553 for writing "On the Errors of the Trinity" by orders from John Calvin.

Unitarians profess a humanist tolerance for all sincere religions and emphasize man's autonomy. Stating that their purpose for uniting is to worship God and to do service to man, they are ready to interact with members of other faiths and often show reverence for leaders of other major religions.

A Unitarian service may follow a formal liturgy or it may be freely composed of hymns, readings from the Bible or non-Christian writings, and communion in memory of Jesus' death. Infant baptism is practiced with water, but no cross is used.

Karl Marx, the father of Communism, called religion "the opium of the people." The Communist Party espouses atheism, which flatly asserts that there is no God. Citizens of Communist-controlled countries are usually allowed, but not encouraged, to worship in their chosen churches and temples.

When we take a look at religion historically and world-wide, we can conclude that most people want to believe that there is some sort of spiritual order to our universe. Albert Einstein said, "I believe in God . . . who reveals Himself in the orderly harmony of the universe." Whether seeking the truth within oneself by meditation, as members of most Eastern religions do, or trying to reach God by the outward performing of good deeds in the world, as the Western traditions generally teach, all seekers want to believe that their individually chosen faith is the correct one that leads to peace and their salvation as humans. And it is. For with the planet becoming more crowded every day as the population increases, it is most essential to our survival that we learn about each person's claim to his own set of beliefs. Ignorance and intolerance go hand-in-hand. We have to be tolerant enough and smart enough to admire the beauty and validity of every set of beliefs, and to minimize the differences among us.

These differences are both the cause and the effect of there being so many hundreds of sects of religion. Although religious expression is diverse throughout the world, there are also many threads that are common to some or all.

Faith in some power greater than man, respect of one's neighbors, belief in the importance of self-knowledge, realization of the need for reciprocity, charity and purification, are basic to many faiths. Best of all, there are tolerance and love, two universal common denominators that encourage mutual understanding and the recognition of every person's right to be a unique seeker of his own particular truth.

Glossary

abode - the place where one lives; home.

A.D. - Latin - Anno Domini - in the year of our Lord; after Christ was born.

adultery - voluntary sex between a married person and a person other than their spouse.

ahimsa - belief in non-violence.

anthropologist - social scientist who studies cultures, races, societies of men.

artifact - that which is man-made; not natural

ascetic - practising strict self-denial as a measure of personal and spiritual discipline.

B.C. - Before Christ

caste - Hindu - hereditary social class.

causality - that which indicates a reason or cause.

consecration - act of inducting a person into an office with a religious rite; making; blessing.

cosmos - the orderly harmonious systematic universe.

dakhma - Parsee - a tower which is open at the top, used for bodies.

deity - god; supreme being.

dharma - Hindu - duty, fulfilled by custom or law.

discerning - understanding.

Druid - ancient Celtic priest.

eminent - standing out as to be easily perceived.

epic - a long poem about a legendary or historical hero.

Epicurean - one who advocates renunciation of momentary pleasure for more permanent pleasure; hedonist; believing that emotional calm equals the highest good.

eschew - to escape; to avoid habitually, especially on moral or practical grounds.

Existentialism - the philosophy which states that there are no positive answers, that you alone are responsible for your experience of existence; empiricism.

fetish - an object believed to have magical powers among primitive peoples.

geomancer - one who foretells the future or discovers hidden knowledge by means of figures, lines, or geographic features.

guru - Hindu - teacher and guide, especially in Sikhism.

Hedonism - the doctrine that pleasure is the chief good in life.

hierarchy - ranked series of those in authority.

immortal - will never die.

Imperialism - policy of extending power of a nation by territorial acquisition or gaining indirect control over political or economic life of other areas.

indigenous - originating in a particular area or environment.

intermediary - mediator; go-between.

lotus position - a sitting position with legs crossed, used for meditation.

megalith - monument, usually made of rough stone.

messiah - expected deliverer of the Jews; the professed or accepted leader of some hope or cause.

moksha - Hindu - eternity; Paradise.

monarchy - government having an hereditary chief of state with life tenure and powers varying from nominal to absolute.

monotheism - worship of one god.

oppressed - burdened by abuse of power of authority.

orthodox - conforming to established doctrine, especially in religion.

pantheism - doctrine that equates God with the forces and laws of the universe; worship of all gods; toleration of worship of all gods.

parable - story that illustrates a moral attitude or religious principle.

phallic - relating to the penis.

pietist - stressing Bible study and personal religious experience.

pilgrimage - journey to a shrine or sacred place.

polygamy - having more than one spouse.

progeny - descendents; children.

prophet - one who speaks divinely inspired revelations.

proselytize - to induce someone to convert to one's faith.

Neo-Platonist - one who believes that the world is an emanation from an ultimate being with whom the soul can be reunited in a trance or ecstasy.

reincarnation - rebirth in a new body or a new form of life.

relief - sculpture in which forms are distinguished from the surrounding plane.

revere - to show honor.

runes - character of an alphabet used for the oldest form of Germanic writing.

Sabbath - seventh day of the week, used for worship and rest.

saffron - orange to orange-yellow

sake - a Japanese alcoholic beverage made of fermented rice.

sauna - Finnish steam bath or dry heat bath.

Shari'a - Islamic code or law.

skald - ancient Scandinavian poet; bard.

Skeptic - one who believes that true knowledge is uncertain.

supernatural - of an existence beyond what is observable.

syncretistic - combining of different forms of belief.

taboo - a prohibition against contact because of dangerous supernatural powers.

temperate - moderate; mild; not extreme.

tenet - principle of belief or doctrine.

transcendental - supernatural; surpassing human experience but not human knowledge.

transvestite - a person, especially a male, who adopts the dress and behavior typical of the opposite sex.

xenophobia - fear of what is foreign.

yin-yang - in Chinese cosmology, combining to produce all that is, by the feminine passive, wet and cold, and the masculine active, dry and warm.

Bibliography

Asimov, Isaac. *Our Human Roots..* New York: Walker Publishing Co., 1979.

Bach, Marcus. *Had You Been Born in Another Faith.* New York: Prentice-Hall, Inc., 1961.

Carmer, Carl. *The Farm Boy and The Angel.* New York: Doubleday, 1970.

Eerdman. *Eerdman's Handbook to the World's Religions.* Herts, England: Lion Publishing, 1982.

Encyclopaedia Americana. Vols. 1, 16, 19, 10. Danbury, Conn.: Grolier, Inc., 1984.

Encyclopaedia Brittanica. Vols. 3, 13, 11, 19, 23, 21, 4, 12, 17. Chicago: Ency. Brit. Inc., 1973.

Encyclopaedia of World Religions. London, England: Octopus Books Ltd., 1974.

Forman, Henry and Gammon, Roland. *Truth is One*. New York: Harper Bros., 1954.

Gaer, Joseph. *How the Great Religions Began*. New York: Signet Books, 1956.

Hultkrantz, Ake. *The Religions of the American Indians*. Berkeley: UC Press

Holy Qur'an, trans. by M.H.Shakir. Elmhurst, N.Y.

Takrike Tarsile Qur'an, Inc., 1984.

Holy Bible, Revised Standard Verson. New York: Thomas Nelson, Inc. 1972.

Jurji, Edward J., Ed. *The Great Religions of the Modern World*. Princeton, N.J.: Princeton Univ. Press, 1946.

Kapoor, Sukhbir S. *Sikhs and Sikhism*. E.Sussex, England: Wayland Publishers, Ltd., 1982.

Langley, Myrtle. *Religions.*

Lanternari, Vittorio. *The Religions of the Oppressed*. New York: Alfred A. Knopf, 1963.

Maulana, Muhammed Ali. *The Religion of Islam*. Lahore, Pakistan: Merza Mohammad Sadiq & Sons, 1983.

Mills, Dorothy M.A. *The Book of the Ancient World.* New York: G.P. Putnam Sons, 1923/1951.

Picken, Stuart D.B.. *Shinto-Japan's Spiritual Roots.* New York: Kodansa Int'l Ltd., 1980.

Ross, Floyd. *Shinto, the Way of Japan.* Boston: Beacon Press, 1965.

Silverberg, Robert. *The Morning of Mankind* New York: N.Y. Graphic Soc. Pub. Inc., 1967.

Thorndike, Joseph J. Jr., Ed. *Discovery - Lost Worlds.* New York: American Heritage Pub. Co. Inc., 1979.

Turville-Petre, E.O.G. *Myth and Religion of the North.* Westport, Conn.: Greenwood Press, 1964.

Van Loon, Hendrik. *The Story of Mankind.* Liveright Publishing Co., 1951.